# Express Yourself

## WRITING SKILLS
## FOR HIGH SCHOOL

▼

Edith N. Wagner

LEARNINGEXPRESS

NEW YORK

Copyright © 2002 LearningExpress, LLC.

All rights reserved under International and Pan-American Copyright Conventions.
Published in the United States by LearningExpress, LLC, New York.

Library of Congress Cataloging-in-Publication Data:
Wagner, Edith N.
  Express yourself : writing skills for high school / by Edith Wagner.
     p. cm.
  ISBN 1-57685-403-5 (alk. paper)
     1. Language arts (Secondary)  2. English language—Composition and exercises.
  I. Title.

LB1631 .W23 2002
  808'.042'0712—dc21                                          2001050445

Printed in the United States of America
9 8 7 6 5 4 3 2 1
First Edition

ISBN 1-57685-403-5

For more information or to place an order, contact LearningExpress at:
 900 Broadway
 Suite 604
 New York, NY 10003

Or visit us at:
 www.learnatest.com

# Contents

# Introduction

Human beings communicate in four ways. We listen, speak, read, and write. When you were a baby the first thing you did was listen to the world around you. You recognized voices; you were startled by noises; you were soothed by music. Then you began to imitate the sounds you heard and you experimented by creating your own sounds. You learned that crying brought attention, words identified things, and that linking words together made meaning. Then you learned that symbols on a page held unique meaning, and you learned to read. The last of the four ways you learned to communicate was through writing, and the very formal transference of words to paper was probably initiated in school, as early as kindergarten.

Now, as adults, even though you can say with confidence that you know "how" to listen, speak, read, and write, you also know that simply knowing *how* doesn't mean you always *do* any one of the four communication strands well. Have you ever "listened" to a lecture and not been able to remember one thing you heard? Have you ever "read" a page or two and had to read it all over again because you didn't concentrate? Have you ever "spoken" and then had to explain something twice because you weren't clear the first time? Have you ever "written" an exam or a paper or even a note, to find you needed some serious help making yourself understood? If you were ever in any of these situations, you were not alone.

Effective communication requires skill—just like mastering a sport, playing an instrument, dancing, cooking, or woodcarving. Communicating well demands that you learn the rules and practice a lot. Now there are many folks out there who get along just fine with basic communication skills, and this book is not for them. This book is for those who want to become more effective at communicating their thoughts and ideas, specifically as writers.

Unlike listening, speaking, and reading, writing is the way we make our thinking visible to the world. Without committing our ideas to paper, our thinking remains invisible, locked in our heads. This is probably a good thing if we are confused or without information. Who would want to put a foolish, illogical, misinformed mind on display for the public? But in today's world of high stakes testing, writing has become the one tried and true measure of your thinking, and everyone wants to see it. So, if you try to avoid writing, this book is dedicated to you.

# How to Use This Book

"High stakes testing" is a phrase that has been captured in the newspapers and has students, parents, and teachers very concerned. Simply defined, high stakes tests are those that have very serious consequences. For example, you are likely to discover that you cannot earn a high school diploma in your state unless you pass certain exit exams. Without that high school diploma, the doors to higher education are locked; entry to certain employment is closed; a career in the military might be impossible. What ties high stakes testing to this book is that all of the tests require you to demonstrate your learning by *writing* what you know in complete sentences. In doing so, you provide a logical pattern of organization that follows the conventions of standard written English. The days of the multiple-choice tests are gone. Testing now wants you to show not just *what* you may know but *how* you know it and how you can *apply* your knowledge and information. In short, today's tests demand that you write.

This book is organized around the four major purposes for writing which drive most of the instruction and all of the testing that you experience in high school and college. The four purposes are:

## WRITING TO DEMONSTRATE INFORMATION AND UNDERSTANDING

This type of writing is also called *expository writing* and it takes the form of your content area term papers and essays. It's where you select information and organize it to show that you understand it. An example would be the social studies essay that asks you to explain the economic, social, and political causes of the Civil War.

## WRITING TO PERSUADE

This type of writing requires that you use information to argue a point and prove it. This kind of writing is often called *writing for critical analysis* because you are asked not only to select appropriate information but also to use that information to prove a point of view. For example, instead of just explaining the causes of the Civil War, you might be asked to persuade your reader that the Civil War was more about the economics of the southern plantation system than it was about the social issue of slavery.

## WRITING TO NARRATE A STORY OR PERSONAL EXPERIENCE

This type of writing requires that you tell a story in order to demonstrate information, knowledge, or personal experience. The same social studies essay would require that you create a series of journal entries written as a plantation owner in 1859 Georgia to demonstrate the social and economic realities of the plantation system, or to construct a chronological narrative of a day in the life of a Confederate soldier.

# WRITING IN RESPONSE TO LITERATURE

This type of writing requires that you read and analyze a piece of literature in one of the four major genres: poetry, prose fiction, prose non-fiction, and drama. You will be asked to respond to questions about the reading and demonstrate an understanding of the text on both a literal and inferential level. Literal questions ask for specific information found directly in the text; inferential questions require that you explain the implied meanings and possible interpretations of the information in the text.

# TIPS FOR SUCCESS

Each section of this book will take you through a complete analysis of each of these writing tasks, explaining how to:

➡ **read** a question to determine what kind of writing is called for and what the main idea of your answer must be.

This is not as easy as it looks. The following question appeared on a recent high school end-of-course test in Global History:

> The Industrial Revolution brought major social and economic changes to Western Europe in the nineteenth century. From your study of global history, choose two European nations and explain how the Industrial Revolution brought both social and economic change to each.

One of the first things you might notice is that this isn't a question at all. Rather, it is a statement of fact, called a *prompt*, which you must support by offering specific details. The prompt asserts the main idea, in this case that the Industrial Revolution brought social and economic change to Western Europe. Is this going to be an essay of information and understanding, persuasion, or narration? If you said, "information and understanding," you were correct. The key word in the prompt is *explain*. You're being asked to identify the main idea, choose two countries, and for each one offer details and examples about the social and economic change brought about by the Industrial Revolution. In short, you're being asked to show that you understand the main idea and that you have supporting details to develop it.

Now look at this prompt from a Life Science exam.

> *Some people claim that certain carnivores should be destroyed because they kill beneficial animals. Explain why these carnivores should be protected and be sure to include information about the population growth of their prey, probability of extinction, and the importance of carnivores in the ecosystem.*

Like the prompt about the Industrial Revolution, this is also a statement question. The main idea is that carnivores should be protected. But unlike the simple statement of fact, this is a statement which contains the word *should*. You are being asked to demonstrate your knowledge by using supporting details to *persuade* the reader that carnivores should be protected rather than destroyed. This is a more difficult task because you must select and evaluate details and data, that will persuade your reader to a certain point of view. In the Industrial Revolution essay you do not have to persuade; you simply have to supply the necessary information to support the statement.

Now try this question from a United States History and Government course:

> *Throughout U.S. history, United States Supreme Court cases have dealt with many major issues. Some major cases are listed below.*
> Marbury v. Madison (1803)
> Korematsu v. United States (1944)
> Brown v. Board of Education (1954)
> Engel v. Vitale (1962)
> Miranda v. Arizona (1966)
> Roe v. Wade (1973)
> Bakke v. University of California (1978)
>
> *Choose three cases and identify the issue in the case; explain the historical circumstances that led to the case; state the Court's decision in the case.*

Is this a prompt based on a statement of fact or a statement of persuasion? Are you being asked to simply provide facts and details or are you being asked to construct an argument that something should or should not happen? If you said "statement of fact," you were right. This is a very straightforward question that wants you to demonstrate knowledge of specific information about Supreme Court decisions.

But it could have been written this way:

> *Throughout U.S. history, the United States Supreme Court has dealt with many major issues. Choose one of the Supreme Court decisions from the following list and explain why you believe it was good or bad for the country.*
> Korematsu v. United States (1803)
> Brown v. Board of Education (1954)
> Miranda v. Arizona (1966)
> Roe v. Wade (1973)
> Bakke v. University of California (1978)

Unlike the previous question, this prompt asks you to take a position and prove it. If you recognized that this was a persuasive essay, you were right on target.

It's not common that a content-specific examination will require you to write a narrative essay. Narration is often used in essays of personal experience such as a college placement essay or a generalized writing test. Narration is easy to spot as a question type because it most often asks you to use "a time" in your life to support an answer. For example:

*People often learn the most about themselves by the mistakes they make. Describe a time in your life when you learned from a mistake.*

OR

*"Problems are opportunities in disguise." Describe a time when you confronted a problem and found that it became an opportunity.*

Both of these are very typical prompts to inspire narrative writing and even though content area assignments could require narrative prose, these would not likely be test questions. However, they still require that you recognize the controlling idea and then use it as the basis of your essay.

As we go through each section of this book, you will be presented with many more opportunities to evaluate question/prompt types. And then you will be shown how to translate the question/prompt to establish the main idea of your essay. You will learn how to:

➡ **write** a statement of purpose to help you prepare the specific information that you will need to support the main idea appropriately.

If you have trouble deciding what the main idea of the question is, then you are having trouble deciding your *purpose* for writing. One way to help you start off on the right foot is to write a statement of purpose. It looks like this:

**My purpose is to** _____ **my audience that** _____ .

Go back to the question and fill in the blanks. For the first example above about the Industrial Revolution, your statement of purpose might look like this:

1. My purpose is to <u>**inform**</u> my audience that <u>**the industrial revolution brought social and economic changes to two European nations in the nineteenth century.**</u>

For the second example about carnivores;

2. My purpose is to <u>**persuade**</u> my audience that <u>**carnivores should be protected.**</u>

For the third example about the Supreme Court cases;

3. My purpose is to <u>**explain**</u> to my audience <u>**the issues, historical circumstances, and decisions of the Supreme Court in these three cases.**</u>

For the fourth example about the Supreme Court cases;

4. My purpose is to <u>**persuade**</u> my audience that <u>**one Supreme Court case was either good or bad for the country.**</u>

You'll notice that once you have restated the question or prompt in this form, you have written out your main idea. Then, and only then, are you ready to:

➡ **decide** the supporting details, examples, and explanations necessary to support that main idea. This is the second stage of planning your essay where you'll have to figure out exactly what information you need so that you don't leave anything out. Very often, content-specific essay questions have more than one part—like the Supreme Court question above or the Industrial Revolution question. To make sure you don't omit anything, you should prepare an outline to follow. This doesn't have to be a formal outline; it could be a graphic organizer. But you should lay out what's required. For example, let's go back to the Supreme Court case question.

My purpose is to explain three court cases for decision, circumstances, and historical significance.

| SUPREME COURT CASE | DECISION | CIRCUMSTANCE | HISTORICAL SIGNIFICANCE |
|---|---|---|---|
| 1. | | | |
| 2. | | | |
| 3. | | | |

This is sometimes referred to as "boxing" the question to make sure you cover all the information that is required.

This *visual organization* strategy is one of several that you'll be shown in the course of this book. Organizers help you in two ways. First, and probably most important, a visual organizer requires that you identify the information that you will use in the essay. If you find that you are missing information, you may change your topic to something about which you are more confident. In the above essay, if you start filling in the boxes and realize you have a blank box because you are unsure of the decision in the Miranda case, then you might go back to choose another case.

The second way that a graphic organizer helps you is that you get to see the paragraph structure of your essay before you start to write. This will help you make sure that your writing is logical and organized. In the Supreme Court case essay, the boxing shows that you will need at least three body paragraphs plus an introduction and conclusion for a total of five paragraphs. But if you felt that you had a lot to say about each case, and if you discovered that you filled each box with so much information that each box represented a paragraph, then this essay could be as many as nine to twelve paragraphs long. See page 141 for a sample essay.

A graphic organizer for the carnivore question might look like this:

| CARNIVORE | POPULATION GROWTH OF THEIR PREY | EXTINCTION | IMPORTANCE TO ECOSYSTEM |
|---|---|---|---|
| | | | |

Once you've laid out the chart you can go back and fill it in. You can see clearly what the question demands. You must identify a specific carnivore on which to base the answer. Then, you must think about specific data pertaining to its population growth, probability of extinction, and its importance to the ecosystem. But there is another element to this essay. Remember the word *should* in the question? You must be sure to include the argument that carnivores should be protected because of the information that you have outlined as important.

How many paragraphs do you think this essay will need? If you said, "three body paragraphs with an introduction and conclusion, for a total of five," you were absolutely right.

As you proceed through the sections of this book you will have several opportunities to practice such pre-writing organization strategies. All of this will lead to the actual writing of the essay and tell you specifically how to:

➡ **write a thesis statement.** *Your thesis statement comes directly from your statement of purpose. It is a single sentence that announces your essay's main idea and organizational pattern. Your thesis statement is the most important part of your answer because it establishes for you and your reader exactly what you will include in the essay and in what order. It is also the first step in your actual writing of your answer, your rough draft.*

A possible thesis statement for the Industrial Revolution question might be:

> *The Industrial Revolution brought both social and economic change to England and France in the nineteenth century because it increased the population of the cities, increased the number of children working in factories, and expanded foreign trade opportunities for both nations.*

By adding the word *because*, the three main points of the essay are established. It is now clear that what will follow will be how the increased population of each city brought social and economic change; how the increased number of children in factories brought social and economic change; how foreign trade increase brought social and political change. Each point will require a full paragraph to develop. Add the introduction and conclusion and you get a five-paragraph essay.

A possible thesis statement for the carnivore essay could be:

> *Wolves are carnivores in need of protection because they control the population of their natural prey, are in danger of extinction, and support the ecosystem in which they live.*

Again, notice the inclusion of the *because* clause. It forces you to be specific about what you will include in your essay. Your job will be to support each of the prongs with specific information and supporting details. In other words, your thesis statement is the main idea of your piece, and that will direct the number and kind of supporting data you need to support it.

As you progress through each section of this book you will have many opportunities to practice writing thesis statements.

Then the last section will help you with the last stage of your writing: proofreading your work for accuracy and correctness.

## KINDS OF QUESTIONS

There are two types of essay questions that will dominate your high school testing experiences.

**Stand-alone prompt:** a topic which requires you to recall the specific data you need to develop a complete, fact-based response.

The social studies essays suggested above are examples of stand-alone prompts. So are the two narrative examples.

**Text-based response:** provides either a reading passage or a series of documents for you to use to support your writing.

This kind of question is often used on major exit exams across the country and is modeled after the Advanced Placement DBQ (document based question). Unlike the stand-alone prompt, this question requires that you read and then select the important information from the given text(s) to use in your answer. It is both a question to test your writing and your reading ability.

Whether the question is *stand-alone* or *text-based,* your response will be graded holistically according to a task-specific rubric. There is an example of this rubric on page 143. Good classroom practice will provide you with a copy of the rubric that enumerates the criteria on which your grade will be based. Often it will be the same rubric that you used throughout a course. Take advantage of this. Know the criteria used to judge your writing so that you can self-revise and self-edit to emphasize the most important criteria.

Whether you're writing a content-based essay or a narrative of personal experience for a college placement essay, there are some general rules to follow that can help you succeed. This book will provide examples and practice activities to help you become familiar with them.

➡ reading the question accurately
➡ deciding on pre-writing strategies
➡ drafting a statement of purpose
➡ drafting a thesis statement
➡ writing a good paragraph
➡ using a rubric

Let's begin!

# WRITING FOR INFORMATION AND UNDERSTANDING

**INFORMATIONAL WRITING** is the process of selecting, combining, arranging, and developing ideas taken from oral, written, or electronically produced texts to demonstrate that you understand and are able to use this information for a variety of rhetorical purposes.

It is important that you understand what is expected before you sit down to write an essay, term paper, or response to an on-demand test prompt. The definition above tells you exactly what is expected for content-area writing that will measure how well you understand information and can reformulate it into your own words for your own purposes. Before we go any further let's define some terms.

*Oral* texts include:
→ speeches
→ video presentations

*Written* texts include:
→ textbooks
→ magazines and newspapers
→ encyclopedias
→ science journals
→ non-fiction books

*Electronically* produced texts include:
→ electronic databases
→ online materials

*Rhetorical* texts include:
→ essays
→ summaries
→ research reports
→ term papers
→ feature articles
→ laboratory observation reports
→ instruction manuals
→ response to on-demand test questions

As you can see, there are many sources from which you can draw upon to demonstrate that you have information and understanding.

There are three chapters in this section. The first two will be geared to reading and writing for information and understanding in school. The third chapter will explore the ways you use this kind of writing in everyday life.

Chapters 1 and 2 will take you through the five important steps in responding to an assignment that asks you to demonstrate information and understanding. They are:

**1.** Reading the assignment to determine your rhetorical purpose.
**2.** Pre-writing to help you organize your ideas.
**3.** Writing a thesis statement.
**4.** Presenting a sample response.
**5.** Evaluating a response from a rubric.

Chapter 3 will explore some of the types of everyday writing you will be asked to do, and it includes techniques on how to accomplish your task easily.

# ONE

# THE TEST QUESTION

**THIS CHAPTER** explains how to break down a

test question to help you be sure that you have

fulfilled all of its requirements.

**A**ll too often students approach a test question by writing down all they know about the general topic. They assume that they will get credit for having some information. But that's not enough to get a good grade or pass an important exam. You also have to be sure you've satisfied the requirements of the question.

For example, look at the following question taken from an end-of-course examination in Earth Science.

**1.** *Earth's climate is in a delicate state of balance and many factors affect it. Describe the way the climate has changed in the past 100 years. Identify two specific reasons for climactic change. Discuss what outcomes in climate change we can predict in the future.*

The first thing you need to do is identify the topic and the main idea of the question. This is clearly stated in the first sentence. The broad topic is *the delicate state of the Earth's climate and the factors that affect it.*

But you can't start writing yet. There are three important words in this question that give you very specific instructions about what you do before you begin. First, the direction is to *describe* the way climate has changed; second, to *identify* two reasons for change; third, to *discuss* predictions for the future. Another way this question could have been asked would be:

2. *Identify three factors that have contributed to climactic changes in the past 100 years. Describe the effects that each has had. Discuss possible future effects.*

You'll notice that in this question you do not have the advantage of having the general topic stated for you. But you can figure it out, and before you go any further in the question that is what you must do. If you said *climate change in the past 100 years,* you would have been correct. Now, you can go ahead and determine the direction words. They are: *identify, describe,* and *discuss.*

Here are some verbs which are commonly used by teachers and test preparers to write essay questions:

| show | describe | explain | identify | contrast |
|------|----------|---------|----------|----------|
| demonstrate | compare | contrast | discuss | list |
| summarize | cite | prove | analyze | evaluate |

For each of the questions below, let's see if you can identify the general topic and then the specific directions which you must follow to get full credit.

3. *Geographic features can positively or negatively affect the development of a nation or a region. Identify three geographic features and show how each had a positive effect on a nation or region other than the United States.*
   ➡ The general topic of this essay is: _____
   ➡ Specific direction words are: _____

4. *What are two different arguments used by some Americans who support unrestricted immigration to the United States? What are two different arguments used by some Americans who support restricted immigration to the United States? Explain each argument and identify at least two specific areas of the world that these arguments mention.*
   ➡ The general topic of this essay is: _____
   ➡ Specific direction words are: _____

5. *In United States history, the rights of "life, liberty, and the pursuit of happiness," as stated in the Declaration of Independence, have been denied to certain groups of Americans. Identify one group of Americans for which these rights have been denied and cite two examples from history to prove this. Show how there have been attempts to correct this injustice.*
   ➡ The general topic of this essay is: _____
   ➡ Specific direction words are: _____

6. *Write an essay explaining two positive and two negative changes in American society as a result of the growth of big business between 1880 and 1920.*

➡ The general topic of this essay is: _____

➡ Specific direction words are: _____

Whether the question is prefaced with an actual topic statement such as questions 1, 2, or 5, or if it's a direct question such as question 4, your first response must be to decide the topic and then the specific directions you must apply to the topic. Sometimes you have to look at the question and figure out the direction words. For example, in question 4, the word *what* is really the direction to *define* or *identify*. Listed below are pairs of question words with their corresponding direction signals.

| | |
|---|---|
| what is/are | define, identify |
| what caused | identify, explain |
| how are/does | explain, evaluate |
| how is *X* like | compare |
| how is *X* different | contrast |
| in what way | illustrate, give examples |
| why is/does | explain |

When you are preparing to answer a test prompt such as the ones above, it may be very difficult for you to realize that you have identified directions for information that you do not have. It's one thing to know that the question needs for you to identify two arguments for unrestricted immigration. It's quite another thing to remember what those arguments are. However, knowing what the question demands can go a long way to help stimulate your memory. And once you do recall information, the question tells you exactly how to use it.

Let's examine a possible response to the social studies question (above) regarding big business and American society between 1880 and 1920.

**TOPIC:** Big business and its effects on American society between 1880 and 1920

**DIRECTION WORDS:** Explain two positive and two negative effects of big business

To be sure you address the question correctly, draw a diagram. Remember the "boxing" technique mentioned in the introduction?

| Changes in society | Positive change | Positive change | Negative change | Negative change |
|---|---|---|---|---|
| America between 1880–1920 | Corporations help build factories | Farm laborers move to cities for new factory jobs | Overcrowded living conditions | Spread of disease due to poor sanitation |

You are now ready to start writing a response. Remember the next step? You need to write a purpose statement.

My purpose in this essay is to <u>*inform*</u> my audience that <u>*big business had two positive and two negative effects on American society between 1880 and 1920*</u>.

The next step is a thesis statement, which comes directly from the purpose statement.

*Big business had two positive and two negative effects on American society between 1880 and 1920* **because** large corporations helped build big, new factories in the cities which created jobs, but they also caused serious overcrowding, poor sanitation facilities, and poor water supplies.

Notice that it is the *because* clause that transforms the statement of purpose into the thesis statement. In other words, by writing *because* you are forced to supply the specific issues that must now be explained using details, examples, and other specific information.

Now try writing the complete essay.

## PRACTICE WRITING

For each of the essay questions below, practice the procedures we've just used. Start by identifying the topic, then isolate the direction words, write the statement of purpose, write the thesis statement, and prepare a box diagram.

1. *Identify three factors which have contributed to climate change in the past 100 years. Describe the effects that each has had. Discuss possible future effects.*

   TOPIC: _____

   DIRECTION WORDS: _____

   Statement of purpose: _____

   _____

   _____

Thesis statement: _____

_____

_____

_____

| Factors that cause climate change | Effects of each change | Future effects of each change |
| --- | --- | --- |
| 1. | 1. | 1. |
| 2. | 2. | 2. |
| 3. | 3. | 3. |

**2.** *Geographic features can positively or negatively affect the development of a nation or a region. Identify three geographic features and show how each had a positive effect on a nation or region other than the United States.*

TOPIC: _____

DIRECTION WORDS: _____

Statement of purpose: _____

_____

_____

Thesis statement: _____

_____

_____

_____

Create your own box diagram:

**3.** *What are two different arguments used by some Americans who support unrestricted immigration to the United States? What are two different arguments used by some Americans who support restricted immigration to the United States? Explain each argument and identify at least two specific areas of the world which these arguments mention.*

TOPIC: _____

DIRECTION WORDS: _____

Statement of purpose: _____

_____

_____

Thesis statement: _____

_____

_____

_____

Create your own box diagram:

**4.** *In United States history, the rights of "life, liberty, and the pursuit of happiness," as stated in the Declaration of Independence, have been denied to certain groups of Americans. Identify one group of Americans for which these rights have been denied and cite two examples from history to prove this. Show how there have been attempts to correct this injustice.*

TOPIC: _____

DIRECTION WORDS: _____

Statement of purpose: _____

_____

_____

**EXPRESS YOURSELF** THE TEST QUESTION

Thesis statement: _____

_____

_____

_____

Create your own box diagram:

Now that you have practiced the essay question type which requires you to respond to what is called a "stand-alone" prompt, it is necessary to look at the question type which provides an actual document or documents to use in your answer. These are called "text-based" questions. These are a very different kind of question—easier in some ways because the information you need is provided for you, but difficult in other ways. For example, despite the fact that the information is in front of you, you have to be able to read it carefully and knowing what to look for helps. The test usually provides this help in the form of a series of multiple-choice questions about the text.

## SCAFFOLD QUESTIONS AND THE TEXT-BASED QUESTION

Did you ever notice the windows being cleaned on very tall buildings? Or the painters working on high bridges? The platforms they construct to support them as they work are called *scaffolds*. The dictionary defines a scaffold as a *supporting framework*. You may be wondering what in the world this has to do with essay writing. Well, in a very real sense the information on which you rest your response is a scaffold. It supports the weight of your answer. If you have weak information—or a weak scaffold—the essay will fall apart just as the window washers or the bridge painters would fall if their supporting scaffold was weak. The *boxing* technique you learned above is a kind of scaffold. If you build a strong box, with accurate and solid information, you will have a strong essay.

When responding to text-based questions, you are usually given a series of multiple-choice questions about the passage(s) to answer before you write. These questions and the answers are intended to direct your attention and your thinking to the information needed for the larger written response. They are called "scaffold" questions because if you use them carefully, they will help you identify exactly what the written response needs to make it not just correct, but strong and well-written.

Your basic plan of attack is the same for the text-based response as it was for the stand alone except you have to add a step: you must read and carefully answer the *scaffold* questions. Here are the steps:

- ➡ Read the text or documents.
- ➡ Answer the multiple-choice questions carefully.
- ➡ Identify the general topic.
- ➡ Identify the direction words.
- ➡ Box or otherwise lay out a diagram of the essay.
- ➡ Write a purpose statement.
- ➡ Write a thesis statement.
- ➡ Write your response.

Let's look at a text-based question from an English/Language Arts exam. The instructions tell you to read and then answer a series of multiple-choice questions before actually writing the essay response. The following question is a very short reading and short essay called an *open-ended* or *short-constructed* response. It is different from a full-length essay because it is designed to measure reading comprehension.

## Question 1

Would you rather live in a big city or out in the country? Read the following passage, answer the questions, and then write a brief explanation about which place the author thinks is best. Be sure to cite at least two reasons for the author's choice.

> *In cities, enormous office buildings rise up to block the light and view. Emissions from traffic, furnaces, and power plants thicken the city air. The constant wail of sirens and the roar of traffic assault auditory nerves and distract attention. No wonder the people who live here become at least nervous, sometimes desperate. Crowded together in these overpopulated centers, we can't sanitarily handle our waste or humanely help the impoverished, the homeless, the insane. Who would want to raise children is such a setting?*

**1.** Which assertion is best supported by the evidence in the above passage?
   **a.** Many poor people live in cities.
   **b.** Cities are not good places to raise children.
   **c.** Ambulance and police sirens make people nervous.
   **d.** Cities are in such bad shape that they are losing population.

**2.** One reason that the author gives for not wanting to live in the city is that
   **a.** people who live in the city become nervous and overwhelmed with life.
   **b.** people who live in the city become impoverished and homeless.
   **c.** loud sounds and awful odors are caused by homeless people.
   **d.** there are too many homeless, insane people in the city and they cause too much noise.

**3.** The word *humanely* means
   a. to treat others with compassion and dignity.
   b. to create sanitariums for the mentally ill.
   c. to leave the city to decide the fate of its people.
   d. to encourage the unemployed to work.

**4.** According to the passage, the author would prefer to live
   a. where people treat each other with dignity and kindness.
   b. where there is good farm land to raise crops.
   c. where there are employment opportunities.
   d. where there is good fire, police, and sanitation service.

Remember the original question? You were directed to read the passage, answer the questions, and then give two reasons why the author thinks the city or the country is the better place to live. Did you notice that the multiple-choice questions helped you look for the answer? The first question asked you to identify the main idea of the passage. Did you say that choice **b** was correct? If so, you were right. Choice **a** is not stated in the text; choice **c** is mentioned in the passage but it is not the main idea; choice **d** is an incorrect conclusion not stated in the passage. Choice **b** is the only one that draws a conclusion based on the details. The last sentence of the passage is actually the topic sentence of the paragraph and could be the thesis statement of a longer essay. So, if you're following the format for answering questions that we laid out before, you have the first part of your answer figured out: the topic.

Question 2 asks for one reason that the author does not want to live in the city. Notice that the question itself directs you to answer the essay piece in a certain way by telling you which place the author thinks is best. If you said choice **a**, you were correct. Choice **b** is not correctly inferred from the passage. It does say that there is poverty and homelessness in the city but it does not say that all people who live in the city become that way. Choices **c** and **d** are not conclusions reached in the passage. Notice that you have one of the two reasons why the author wants to live in the country, and you can use this for your written response.

Question 3 asks for you to figure out the meaning of the word *humanely*. If you said choice **a**, you were correct. Choices **b**, **c**, and **d** are simply incorrect based on the main idea of the passage. Notice that this response helps you define a second reason for the author's preference to live in the country. If not being able to treat people in a humane way—with dignity and compassion—is a negative fact of city life, then it is a reason to live in the country. See how the question leads you to the essay answer?

Question 4 is yet another helping hand for you. If you chose **a**, then you actually have the concluding sentence for your essay. Choices **b**, **c**, and **d** may all be true, but they aren't mentioned in the essay.

Let's go back and look at the directions for the original question and follow the plan for answering questions.

**1.** We read the question and text(s).
**2.** We answered the multiple-choice questions.
**3.** We identified the topic as *city life vs. country life.*
**4.** We decided direction words were *explain* and *cite two reasons.*
**5.** We boxed the question.

| Country or city | Reason 1 | Reason 2 |
|---|---|---|
| The quality of life is better in the country. | Loud noises make people nervous. | People treat people with dignity and respect |

6. We determined our purpose was to explain two reasons why the author thinks the country is a better place to live than the city.

7. The author thinks the country is a better place to live than the city because loud noises make people nervous, and he'd rather live in a place where people treat other people with dignity and compassion.

8. Here is our sample response:

> *In the passage above the author would rather live in the country than in the city. Two important reasons are that loud noises make people nervous, and in the city, people do not treat others with respect and dignity. The author would rather live in a place where people treat each other with dignity and compassion and where there is peace and quiet.*

This short written response, also called a *short-constructed response*, is often graded on a four-point scale. To get four points you have to answer the question completely, accurately, and correctly. The short answer above would get four points.

But the following answer would only get one point.

> *The author says he'd rather live in the country because it is a nicer place.*

The writer will get one point for correctly identifying that the author would prefer the country to the city. However, each reason is worth one point, and the writer did not identify any reasons, such as loud noise, air pollution, overpopulation, or waste removal, that were specifically stated in the passage so he lost two points; he lost the fourth point because he did not provide any explanation other than the overly general statement that the country is "nicer."

Now try this question based on the passage that follows. This passage is longer and more specific but it is also a text-based response question. It requires two short, open-ended responses, which are just short written answers rather than one longer essay. Most of the new high school exit exams—the ones you need to pass in order to graduate from high school—use both types of text-based questions. They include both short and long texts with the question format that asks you to answer scaffold questions and then write your response. These questions measure not only your ability to write but also your ability to read and identify important information in a fiction or non-fiction text.

## Question 2

The pyramid for healthy food choices is an important tool for helping us maintain healthy bodies. Read the passage below and answer the questions that follow.

> *Although more and more people are exercising regularly, experts note that eating right is also a key to good health. Nutritionists recommend the food pyramid for a simple guide to eating the proper*

*foods. At the base of the food pyramid are grains and fiber. You should eat six to eleven servings of bread, cereal, rice, and pasta everyday. Next up the pyramid are vegetables and fruit; five to nine daily servings from this group are recommended. The next pyramid level is the dairy group. Two to three servings a day of milk, yogurt, or cheese help maintain good nutrition. Moving up the pyramid, the next level is the meat, poultry, fish, beans, eggs, and nuts group, of which everyone should eat only two to three servings a day. At the very top of the pyramid are fats, oils, and sweets; these foods should be eaten only infrequently.*

*You don't have to shop in health food stores to follow the guidelines. One easy way to plan menus that follow the food pyramid is to shop only in the outer aisles of the grocery store. In most supermarkets, fresh fruit and vegetables, dairy, fresh meat, and frozen foods are in the outer aisles of the store. Grains, like pasta, rice, bread, and cereal, are located on the next aisles, the first inner rows. Finally, the farthest inside the store is where you'll find chips and snacks, cookies and pastries, soda pop and drink mixes. These are the kinds of foods that nutritionists say everyone should eat rarely, if at all. If you stay in the outer aisles of the grocery store, you won't be tempted to buy foods you shouldn't eat, and you will find a wide variety of healthy foods to choose from. Another benefit of shopping this way is that grocery shopping takes less time.*

**1.** A good title for this article would be
   a. How to Shop in a Health Food Store.
   b. How to Shop Efficiently.
   c. How to Shop for Healthy Food.
   d. How to Cook Healthy Food.

**2.** According to the passage, the best way to shop in a grocery store is to
   a. make a list and stick to it.
   b. stay in the outer aisles.
   c. stay in the inner aisles.
   d. check the newspaper ads for bargains.

**3.** According to the food pyramid, people should
   a. eat more grains than meat.
   b. never eat fats and sweets.
   c. eat mostly vegetarian meals.
   d. rarely eat bread and other starches.

**4.** According to the passage, on the inner aisles of the grocery store you will find
   a. cleaning products.
   b. dog and cat food.
   c. wine and beer.
   d. chips and snacks.

**5.** According to the passage, to maintain good health, people should
   a. buy their food in health food stores.
   b. worry more about nutrition than exercise.
   c. exercise and eat right.
   d. eat from the top of the food pyramid.

**6.** In order to follow the main advice in the passage, it would be most helpful to know
   a. where to purchase a copy of "The Food Pyramid."
   b. whether rice has more calories than pasta.
   c. which supermarket the author is referring to.
   d. how much of each kind of food equals a serving.

**7.** The purpose of this passage is to
   a. persuade.
   b. inform.
   c. entertain.
   d. narrate.

**8.** This passage is based on
   a. opinion.
   b. fact.
   c. outdated information.
   d. predictions for the future.

## Open-ended questions

Answer the following two questions using information from the passage above. Write complete sentences.

**1.** What evidence does the author provide to support his position that it is healthier to shop the outer aisles of the grocery store?

_____

_____

_____

_____

**2.** Explain why the author would suggest that everyone have a copy of the food pyramid in his or her home.

_____

_____

_____

_____

**EXPRESS YOURSELF** THE TEST QUESTION

See page 145 for possible answers.

Still a third type of text-based question is the one where you may be given two or more short texts, including a diagram, chart, or other visual. You will be asked to answer short scaffold questions following each text. Then, using your answers to the scaffold questions, you will respond to a more complete essay question. This is called a *document-based question*, similar to the Advanced Placement exam format. The following question was taken from a state exit exam.

Read the texts on the following pages, answer the scaffold questions, and write a response based on the task described at the end of the documents.

## Document 1

The average. . . . Japanese consumes 10 times as much of the world's resources as the average Bangladeshi. Japan and Bangladesh have the same [number of people] but [these people] have a vastly different effect on their ecosystems [environments].

—The "Living Planet" Report

**1a.** How does Japan's use of resources differ from Bangladesh's use of resources?

_____

_____

**1b.** What is the reason for this difference?

_____

_____

## Document 2

Rich nations point out that developing countries, while responsible for just 26 percent of carbon emissions since 1950, are quickly becoming major emitters in their own right. And, as industrial countries emphasize, booming populations and economic growth are fueling an explosive increase in carbon emissions. The United States Department of Energy projects that carbon output from developing nations will, in the absence of any new policies, outgrow that of their neighbors as early as 2020, with China eclipsing the United States as the world's leading emitter by 2015.

—*World Watch*, 1998

**2a.** What concern about the future of the environment is being expressed in this document?

_____

_____

**2b.** According to the document, what current trends have caused the United States Department of Energy to make this projection?

_____

_____

## Document 3

➡ British Petroleum President John Browne surprised the oil industry when he announced last year . . . BP's intention to step up investments in solar energy.

➡ Toyota stunned the auto world with the delivery to its showrooms of the world's first hybrid electric car—with twice the fuel economy and half the $CO_2$ [carbon dioxide] emissions of conventional cars.

➡ After a decade of effort, Denmark now generates [some] of its electricity from wind power and . . . from the combustion of agricultural wastes.
　　—_World Watch_, November/December 1998

**3.** Identify two ways that nations or corporations of the world are responding to environmental problems.

_____

_____

_____

_____

_____

## Document 4

The United States and 34 other industrial countries met in Rio de Janiero, Brazil, to discuss world environmental concerns.

Rio Pact 1992

Agenda 21

The Agenda establishes the following priorities for international environmental action:

➡ achieving sustainable growth, as through integrating environment and development in decision making

➡ making the world habitable by addressing issues of urban water supply, solid waste management, and urban pollution

→ encouraging efficient resource use, a category which includes management of energy resources, care and use of fresh water, forest development, management of fragile ecosystems, conservation of biological diversity, and management of land resources

→ protecting global and regional resources, including the atmosphere, oceans and seas, and living marine resources

→ managing chemicals and hazardous and nuclear wastes

**4.** Identify two environmental issues discussed at the Rio Conference.

_____

_____

_____

_____

_____

## Task

Using information from the documents, write an essay in which you discuss the problems that industrialization has caused in the nations of the world. Explain how nations are responding to these problems. Support your response with relevant facts, examples, and details from at least four of the documents.

Notice that this question is more complex and requires more reading than some of the previous examples. Practice the techniques we learned:

**1.** Read the texts.
**2.** Answer the scaffold questions. Did you notice that the answers to the questions provide the paragraph structure for your essay?
**3.** Identify the topic.
**4.** Identify the direction words.
**5.** Box the question. Use your answers to the scaffold questions for your boxes.
**6.** Write a purpose statement.
**7.** Write a thesis statement with a *because* clause.
**8.** Write your essay being sure to have an introduction and at least three body paragraphs with a conclusion.

See page 145 for a sample response.

Now that you have practiced reading and writing for information and understanding as they relate to test questions, let's look at reading and writing for information in term paper assignments.

# TWO

# THE TERM PAPER ASSIGNMENT

**THIS CHAPTER** explains how to analyze and get ready for a term paper assignment. You will learn to define a topic, develop a thesis statement, prepare an organization plan, and identify the need for specific information.

Now that you are familiar with reading and writing for information and understanding as demanded by important test situations, it's time to examine the second most important way that you are asked to perform to that standard: researching and writing the term paper.

Many teachers will assign a research paper using broad topic guidelines. For example, you may be asked to write a research paper in a health class with a very open assignment such as:

Prepare a 750–1,000 word research paper on any of the following topics:

Teenage smoking

Panic disorders

Marijuana use

A current health issue

Pollution

Your paper must use at least three sources to provide current details and evidence to support your paper.

Depending on the length of the paper and the weight it will have in determining your course grade, you may be required to use more than three sources. For right now, let's work with the assignment above.

## FROM TOPIC TO THESIS

The first thing you need to know is that a topic is only the beginning of your efforts. The first thing you have to think about is what you're going to say about your topic. Remember the example of the students who just wrote everything they knew about the subject of the question and hoped to get some points? Well, that can happen on term paper assignments, too. But if you want a really good grade, you have to be sure that doesn't occur.

Start by choosing a topic in which you have some interest or even personal experience. A good way to brainstorm what you already know or think is to make a list. The topic "Teenage Smoking" may be very important to you because even at age sixteen or seventeen you may be struggling with trying to quit; or you may have experienced a loved one's struggle with lung cancer or heart disease related to cigarette smoking; or, as a non-smoker you may be really upset with the discourtesy of your peers who violate the air space in your common areas by smoking.

Your first brainstorm list might look like this:

➡ quitting the habit
➡ smoking makes you sick
➡ secondhand smoke is disgusting

As you go on with the list, other things might come into your mind:

➡ smokers' rights
➡ tobacco settlement money
➡ teenagers have rights

But you still have only topics. So, let's choose one that you know something about or may even have some interest in learning about. One of the most important aspects of successful research is that you are interested in your topic.

Because you are struggling to quit smoking you have decided to use this term paper assignment to help you figure out why it's so hard. Maybe you might even get some tips on how to be more successful at it. Thus, your brainstorm list of possible topics becomes:

➡ the negative health effects of teenage smoking
➡ teenage smoking and the difficulties of quitting
➡ teenage smoking and how to quit
➡ teenage smoking and why quitting is important

These are four possible topic statements that you can now convert into purpose statements. Remember purpose statements? They help you define who and what you are writing for.

*My purpose is to inform my teacher that teenage smoking has negative effects.*

So far, so good. But do you remember what comes next? You still only have a topic. The *because* clause is next, it signals your thesis statement. But in order to write an effective thesis statement you have to have at least three ideas and you may not have those yet. So the first thesis statement you try to write may only be the beginning of your work.

*Teenage smoking has negative effects because it is addictive; it causes long term, serious health problems; it costs the taxpayers money.*

From this thesis statement you can *box* or otherwise lay out your paper's research needs. This time instead of a box, let's try a more conventional outline.

**TEENAGE SMOKING**

I.   Introduction
II.   One negative effect is addiction, not habit.
    A.   first fact related to addiction
    B.   second fact related to addiction
III.   Negative effect two is long-term health consequences.
    A.   lung diseases
    B.   heart diseases
IV.   Negative effect three is the cost to taxpayers.
    A.   how much
    B.   why is this bad
V.   Conclusion

This is a very incomplete outline but it provides a basic structure and direction for your work. Do you notice how each of the roman numerals (I–V) corresponds to a subsection of your paper? If your paper is between 750–1000 words, plan to have each Roman numeral and each subject heading as a complete paragraph. Each idea must be fully developed. In other words, the structure of your paper is determined by how much information you have to include.

For this paper, which is only 750–1,000 words (average page length is 250 words per page), and requires only three reference sources, your outline tells you that you have to provide information—including details, facts, data—in three areas: addiction, health, and taxpayer cost. Suddenly you know exactly what information you need for your paper. When you finally go online or to the library for research, your work has been streamlined. Instead of floundering through information looking for what *might* be helpful, you can search for *exactly* what you need. All too often students start research before they have identified their needs. They download pages and pages of information related to their topic rather than their thesis statement.

Sometimes you are given a general topic and no matter how hard you try to come up with a tentative thesis statement it just isn't there. You may want to request a conference with your teacher, or you may need to discuss the topic with a friend or parent. Or, you may have to do some preliminary reading/research to come up with an approach to your topic. As a matter of fact, thesis statements often come after preliminary research. You may need to read an article or two to see what information is available.

For example, let's go back to the smoking topic and health risks. You really don't know much about the topic and you never gave much thought to how serious the health risks might be. So you go online and do a general search of teen smoking. One of the articles that catches your attention is "Quit Selling Cigarettes to Kids." As you read the article, you notice that the author says that tobacco sales to teenagers should be subject to state law because the health threat to them is so serious. You then read another article that talks about "smokeless" tobacco. This opens an entirely new avenue of research because you never realized that chewing tobacco is almost as dangerous as smoking it. Suddenly you become very alert to information in many different places that enumerate many different negative consequences of tobacco products especially as they affect the health of teenagers. You start a *map* of your subject, which looks like this:

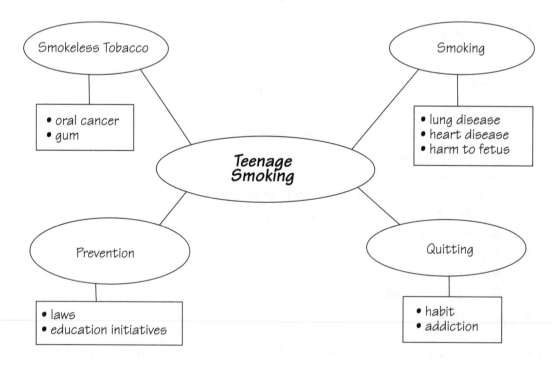

**EXPRESS YOURSELF** THE TERM PAPER ASSIGNMENT

Suddenly, a thesis statement seems possible:

*Teenage smoking has long-term consequences which will cause irreparable harm because tobacco is an addictive substance that causes major organ damage such as heart disease as well as oral cancers.*

An outline map can easily be developed from this thesis statement.

I.      Introduction
II.     Main idea one: nicotine is addictive
        Supporting details
        1.
        2.
III.    Main idea two: organ damage (heart and lung)
        Supporting details for heart
        1.
        2.
        Supporting details for lung
        1.
        2.
IV.     Main idea three: oral cancer and smokeless tobacco
        Supporting details for smokeless tobacco
        1.
        2.
V.      Conclusion

Now it's just a matter of picking and choosing your details. If your thesis has evolved from your research you probably have kept track of your sources by jotting down the important information you will need to credit them. For instance, you will have noted the author's name, the publication title, the date of publication and the page numbers.

This leads you to choosing the research data to support your main points. Once you have decided what information you already have or need to find, you must be very careful to attribute your data to the source from which you received it.

## PARAPHRASING/SUMMARIZING/QUOTING

There are three ways for you to use information, data, details, facts, and figures that you may have discovered in your research. Paraphrasing and summarizing are similar. They both involve putting someone else's ideas into your own words. But you must still identify the person from whom you borrowed the information.

For example, if you're going to rely on data from the United States Department of Health and Human Services—that gave you the number $52 billion a year in health related costs for smokers—then you will want to be sure to *signal* the reader that this specific information was provided by them.

> *According to the United States Department of Health and Human Services, $52 billion each year is spent by Americans in costs related to the negative health consequences of cigarette smoking.*

If this were a direct quote from a journal article or textbook you would write:

> *According to John Smith, a noted physician, "$52 billion each year is the cost borne by American citizens ravaged by the effects of cigarette smoking."*

In either case, you must have a correct *citation* for your work and your teacher will direct you to the proper use of either APA or MLA format. Both formats require you to include the author and title of the article, the title of the publication in which your reference appears, the year of its publication, the place of its publication, and the page number where it can be located. Be sure you record this information as you progress through your work. It's very time-consuming and frustrating to lose track of a reference and have to spend valuable time retracing your steps.

## CRITERIA FOR EVALUATING YOUR WORK

You've probably heard the word "rubric" many times. Most likely, you've worked with a rubric in your English classes. A rubric is a chart that identifies the criteria against which your essay writing is scored. Usually, rubrics work on either a 1–4 or a 1–6 scale with 1 being the lowest score. The following characteristics are used as the basis for almost all the scoring charts used for essay writing:

### Establish focus by asserting a main or controlling idea.

A main, or controlling, idea is your *thesis statement* or what you have to say about the topic.

### Develop content using sufficient and appropriate supporting details.

Developing the content of your essay or term paper using *sufficient* and *appropriate* details means that you followed the assignment to include the required *number of references* and that you chose data, facts, examples, and reasons specific to your *content*. These should support your main idea (thesis) about the topic.

### Provide a logical pattern of organization.

A logical pattern of organization shows that the *paragraphs* you developed follow your thesis statement.

### Convey a sense of style with the use of varied vocabulary and sentences.

Sense of style refers to your ability to write more than simple sentences; varied vocabulary means that you do not keep using the same words and phrases over and over again.

# *Demonstrate control of the conventions of standard written English.*

The conventions of standard written English refers to the rules of grammar. Did you write in complete sentences? Did you use punctuation correctly? Do you have too many spelling errors?

A rubric sets all this up in chart form and looks something like this:

| | FOCUS | CONTENT | ORGANI-ZATION | STYLE | CONVENTIONS |
|---|---|---|---|---|---|
| **4** | Sharp, distinct, controlling main point made about a single topic with evident awareness of task; thesis is clear. | Substantial, specific and/or illustrative content demonstrating development and support of thesis. | Sophisticated arrangement of content into clearly developed paragraphs with appropriate transitions. | Careful choice of words and sentence structure to support and highlight purpose and tone. | None or only one or two errors in grammar, spelling, or sentence usage. |
| **3** | Apparent main point made about a single topic with sufficient awareness of task; thesis is adequate. | Sufficiently developed content with adequate use of details related to the main idea. | Adequate arrangement of content into paragraphs that follow the main idea; some transitions. | Adequate choice of words; basic but repeated sentence structure. | Errors in grammar, spelling, usage that do not interfere with communication of ideas. |
| **2** | Single topic is identified but no main point or thesis established. | Limited content; details not all related to main idea. | Confused arrangement of content; paragraphs do not establish a logical pattern of organization; no transitions. | Poor choice of vocabulary; weak but grade appropriate sentence structure. | Errors in grammar, spelling, usage somewhat interfere with communication. |
| **1** | Minimal evidence of topic; no main idea or thesis. | No details specific to a main idea; no explanation of details as they relate to topic. | No control of paragraphs; no transitions. | Poor choice of vocabulary; weak and grade inappropriate sentence structure. | Errors in grammar, spelling, usage interfere with communication. |

Once you have written a paper, it is always a good idea to have a second reader go over your work to be sure you haven't overlooked any obvious errors. However, working with the criteria chart can help you and your reader be on the lookout for areas of improvement in the meaning and logic of your piece. It is much easier to spot errors in spelling than errors in logic or paragraph unity. You will notice that in the way the rubric is arranged, the most important aspects of your writing are on the top. This is not to say that mechanics are not important, but content and organization are always the most important parts of writing for information and understanding. They are the way you make it clear to your reader/evaluator that you have understood the task, identified the important elements of information needed to explain the task, and organized the information into a logically ordered written presentation.

A sample essay and explanation of how it would be scored can be found on pages 146-147.

Not all reading and writing for information and understanding is related to test questions and term paper assignments. Now let's take a look at how this kind of expository writing impacts your everyday life.

# THREE

# EVERYDAY WRITING

**THIS CHAPTER** explains some of the everyday purposes that apply to reading and writing for information and understanding. You will learn how to apply the skills you have just learned to write business letters, directions/instructions, and general summaries.

Just how does writing which seems so geared to school have any connection to your everyday life? You may even be thinking that once you're out of school you'll never have to write again. Well, that's simply not the case. With e-mail developing as a primary means of everyday communication, writing to communicate information and demonstrate understanding is of major importance.

This is especially true as you enter the business world and hope to climb the corporate ladder. Remember what we said at the very beginning of this book? "Writing is the way we make our thinking visible to the world." Consider then the likelihood that your boss or business manager would want to promote you to a leadership position if he or she hasn't seen a particularly clear and organized mind. And we're not talking about waiting until you're out of college or graduate school. Even if you're just working your way through school waiting until you can finally land the job of your dreams, your writing can establish you as a competent, confident individual worthy of responsibility.

Here are some of the most important characteristics of business writing in general, and e-mail in particular:

➡ Know your audience.
➡ Anticipate your audience's needs and questions.
➡ State your main idea in the opening sentence.
➡ Be brief. Avoid wordy, repetitive writing.
➡ Avoid slang, buzz words, jargon, and colloquialisms.
➡ Never include jokes, clichés, and ethnic references.
➡ Be factual, not emotional.
➡ Focus on the positive by choosing positive words and phrases.
➡ Always proofread to be sure that you have followed the conventions of standard written English. Even in e-mail: correct grammar— including capitalization and diction—apply.

Let's look at each of these and see how they actually affect business writing. First, the concept of knowing your audience is important no matter what your purpose for writing. In the case of the business memo or letter, knowing your audience will determine how much information you need to provide, and what specific questions and/or needs will have to be addressed. For example, your manager has asked that you e-mail the other employees about the annual Memorial Day picnic. You could write:

To:       Everybody
From:   Chuck
Re:       Our annual picnic

The Memorial Day picnic is going to be at Sherwood Park on Monday. Mark Manager asked me to invite you guys.

Bring burgers and stuff and get ready for a blast!

See ya

The response to your e-mail is slow and steady. You are asked by all of the people you e-mailed what time they should come and what they should bring other than their own burgers. Or did you mean that everyone should simply supply everything, including soda and chips and paper goods. And exactly what did you mean by a blast? Last year there was an organized volleyball game. Is that happening again this year? Should they bring volleyballs? You know all the answers and by the time you have recited them all for the fourteenth time you are behind in your work and not at all sure if anyone will actually attend the picnic. Mark Manager isn't too happy with you either. He's heard from several people that the e-mail *he* sent was confusing. Apparently, some people assumed that it was his invitation because he's the boss.

So what went wrong? First, you wrote for an audience that you assumed had the same background information that you did. They were all there last year. Right? Wrong. There were several old-timers who missed last year, and there are at least three new people who had no previous experience. Second, for everyone concerned, dates (not just Monday), times (from 3 to midnight), and location (specific street) would have been helpful. Third, you said bring "burgers." Did that mean that the company was providing everything else?

Mark Manager is right to think that you didn't give much thought or planning to this task. So he rewrote the memo.

TO:      All employees, families and friends
FROM:   Mark Manager
RE:      Annual Memorial Day Picnic

Please plan to attend our Memorial Day Picnic on Monday, May 25th, at Sherwood Park from 3PM to midnight. A direction map is attached for those of you who are new to our company.

We'll provide all the beverages and paper goods but the food is up to you. Please bring enough food, snacks, et cetera for your own group. As always, family and friends are welcome.

We need a head count, so let me know by Friday, the 22nd how many you'll be bringing.

We will have our annual volleyball tournament! Come ready to have a good time!

Notice that Mark Manager will not have to take time away from the important work of everyday business—where time means money and productivity—to answer questions. His memo anticipated and answered the most important questions.

Another example of everyday writing that you might confront is the message to your teacher or school district administrator requesting resolution to a complaint or requesting information. For example, Sally Student was very unhappy with her final grade in science. She spoke to her teacher but someone told her that when you put something in writing it is always taken more seriously. Thus Sally decided to write to Mrs. Biology.

Dear Mrs. Biology,

I really don't think my grade was fair and I want you to recalculate it and change it if you can.

Thanks a lot.

Sally

Mrs. Biology receives this letter and wonders:

➡ Sally who?
➡ What class was she in?
➡ What grade is she complaining about? Was it the final exam or the final grade?

➡ What does she expect me to do?

➡ Boy, does this student have an "attitude."

When Sally gets no response, her friend who got an A+ in English, helps her re-write the letter.

1010 Grade Point Avenue
Transcript City, New York
June 15, 2001
Dear Mrs. Biology,

I was a student in your Biology 103 class this past semester. When I received my final grade of C+ I was very disappointed. I had expected a B. I calculated my grades as follows:

| | |
|---|---|
| mid-term | 87 |
| term paper | 89 |
| quizzes | 83 |
| final | 77 |

I believe that each grade was 25% of the grade so averaged out that would have been an 84 or a B.

I would appreciate it if you would get back to me as soon as possible and let me know if a mistake was made.

Thank you,

Sally Student

An e-mail would have been similar in format, but the heading would have been different:

TO:       Mrs. Biology
FROM:     Sally Student
RE:       Final Grade
DATE:     June 3, 2001

I was a student in your Biology 103 class this past semester. When I received my final grade of C+ I was very disappointed. I had expected a B. I calculated my grades as follows:

| | |
|---|---|
| mid-term: | 87 |
| term paper: | 87 |
| quizzes: | 83 |
| final: | 77 |

I believe that each grade was 25% of the final grade so averaged out that would have been an 84 or a B.

I would appreciate it if you would get back to me as soon as possible and let me know if a mistake was made.

Thank you,

Sally Student

Whether e-mail or snail mail (a slang term for regular mail), the revisions accomplished three very important goals of good business writing: tone, clarity, and expectation.

# TONE

Mrs. Biology was right to question Sally's "attitude." In the first memo Sally was accusatory. It is clear she thinks Mrs. Biology made a mistake and she is essentially demanding that Mrs. Biology correct it. In both revisions, the accusation is gone and a question replaces it. Was an error made and could it have been Sally's? This leaves Mrs. Biology the opportunity to correct Sally's or her own mistake without being defensive.

Word choice creates positive tone. See if you can tell the difference between these sentences.

| | |
|---|---|
| You made a mistake. | An error has been made. |
| You failed to appear. | You weren't present. |
| That's going to be a problem. | That will be a real challenge. |
| You didn't include your check. | Your check was not included. |
| Turn in your paper on time. | Papers are due on Monday. |

In each of the above pairs, the sentence in the right hand column is more positive than its counterpart in the left hand column. You may think this is only *playing* with words, but word choice conveys attitude. You never want to create a negative attitude when you want something accomplished. In the first pair, the word "mistake" is more negative than the word "error" and declaring that "you" made it is an accusation. On the other hand, saying that an error "was made" leaves out the blame.

In the second set, the word "failed" is replaced with "weren't present." No one likes to be told they "failed" anything. In the third, "problems" always sound insurmountable and difficult. "Challenges" imply satisfaction and accomplishment. In the fourth, rather than saying "you" didn't do something, the burden was shifted to the check. Again, the reader doesn't feel personally attacked. In the fifth, the command to turn in your paper was softened by making the request more general.

Word choice and word order are the key elements in creating positive tone. See what you can do to rewrite and improve the tone of the following:

**1.** Send an application immediately. _____

**2.** You have not sent the college catalog I requested. _____

**3.** I expect that you will correct the mistake on my transcript. _____

**4.** You are expected to be in class on time and prepared to work. _____

**5.** All employees must be dressed in clean clothes. _____

See page 147 for suggested answers.

## CLARITY

Clarity is simply making sure that the problem is clearly presented. That usually means including those famous 5 *w*'s: *who, what, when, where, why,* and *how.* Going back to the revision of Sally's letter, she gives Mrs. Biology enough information to identify her, her class, her numerical grades, and how she calculated the final grade she expected. She anticipated Mrs. Biology's needs—she saved her time and made it easier for her to respond to Sally quickly and correctly.

## EXPECTATION

Sally has also made clear what she expects to happen as a result of her request. She expects to receive an answer and possibly a recalculation of her grade. Furthermore, she has provided her street address or her e-mail address for Mrs. Biology.

Tone and clarity are very important elements in good business writing. Whether you're asking for information or for help of any kind, you must be polite, direct, and clear.

Following is a list of everyday purposes for writing. Try writing these letters and e-mails.

**1.** Write a letter to your building principal inviting him to be a guest speaker in your economics class. Remember the 5 *w*'s.
**2.** Write an e-mail to your English teacher asking for help with an assignment. Be specific about what you need to know. You can make up an assignment appropriate to your grade or subject.
**3.** Write a letter responding to an ad in the paper for an after school job at a local store. Make up a store where you've always wanted to work.
**4.** Write directions to your house for a friend who will be visiting from school. Remember, he's never been to your house before.
**5.** You recently purchased a DVD and it doesn't play. The store told you to "put it in writing." Write a letter of complaint.

# TWO

# WRITING TO PERSUADE

Persuasive writing is the process of selecting, combining, arranging, and developing ideas taken from oral, written, or electronically produced texts for the purpose of arguing a point of view or convincing an audience to take action. Persuasive writing is often called argumentation.

This may sound like writing for information and understanding, but persuasive writing uses information for a specific purpose and that is to convince your audience to accept your point of view or your call to action. You are still going to use the same sources for information: oral, written, and electronic. But your rhetorical tasks will be somewhat different. Listed below are some of the tasks that fall under the category of persuasive.

➡ persuasive essays
➡ thesis/support research papers that argue a point of view
➡ editorials
➡ book and movie reviews
➡ literary critiques
➡ speeches to persuade
➡ debates

Even though speeches and debates fall under "speaking" not "writing," only the impromptu speech is not written out before it is delivered. Both persuasive writing and speaking require the same attention to the selection of effective details and organization. So we will also explore oral persuasion strategies.

There will be three chapters to this section. Chapter 4 will cover how to write a comprehensive thesis statement for argumentation and will examine research techniques and the selection of materials for persuasion. Chapter 5 will explore oral persuasion skills. Chapter 6 will show how all of this carries over into your everyday life.

Chapter 4: Thesis Statements and Effective Research
Chapter 5: Writing for Persuasive Speaking
Chapter 6: Persuasion in Everyday Writing

Let's begin!

# FOUR

# THESIS STATEMENTS AND EFFECTIVE RESEARCH

**THIS CHAPTER** explains the difference between claims of fact and claims of persuasion. You will learn how to write an effective thesis statement and integrate it into a powerful introduction. Then you will learn how to select information and present it to win your audience to your side.

For example, writing for information follows from a claim of fact. The following statements are claims of fact as presented by the Environmental Protection Agency:

1. Each person generates more than four pounds of garbage each day of his or her life.
2. In America, 1,500 aluminum cans are recycled every second.
3. Eighty-five percent of our garbage is sent to the landfill, where it can take from 100–400 years for things like cloth and aluminum to decompose.

**4.** Americans receive almost four million tons of junk mail a year.

**5.** Americans throw away the equivalent of more than 30 million trees in newsprint each year.

The above statements are facts. They represent information about the topic "Pollution." You can write a term paper about pollution and use these five pieces as major points of information to support a thesis statement such as:

American consumption is environmentally hazardous because we are destroying our forests, wasting our water, and polluting our air.

But if you were to write a persuasive paper to argue that not only is consumption hazardous but that it also must be reduced, then your statements of facts would be used to support a thesis that says that something *should be done* about that consumption—that is, it should be reduced. You are taking a position *about* your subject and you would be attempting to convince your audience that you are right. A thesis statement would read:

American consumption is environmentally hazardous and we should reduce, reuse, and recycle our trash or we will destroy our environment.

The difference between the two thesis statements should be clear to you. The statement of fact simply states that consumption is hazardous; the statement of persuasion tells what must be done to change or improve it. Both thesis statements can use the facts above, but the persuasive paper will use the facts to convince the reader to take specific and immediate action.

Another example might be:

**1.** Auto accidents involving cell phone use have increased tenfold in the past two years.

**2.** Many local governments are now enacting laws to prohibit cell phone use while driving.

**3.** Many restaurants post signs reminding customers to turn off their cell phones while dining.

**4.** An exit poll of moviegoers in New Jersey revealed that one in four had had a movie interrupted by the ringing of a cell phone.

**5.** Airlines require cell phones to be shut off when in flight because the signals can create flight risks.

Use these facts to create a thesis statement for an informative paper. _____

_____

_____

_____

_____

Now create a thesis statement for a persuasive paper. _____

_____

_____

_____

_____

**EXPRESS YOURSELF** THESIS STATEMENTS AND EFFECTIVE RESEARCH

Here's what you might have written.

Cell phone use is being restricted in many places because it creates safety and courtesy problems.

This is a simple statement of fact. On the other hand:

New Jersey should pass strict laws regulating the use of cell phones because they pose great safety risks and they ruin leisure-time activities.

Do you see that the first thesis does not make a value judgment about cell phone use? It simply says that cell phones are being restricted and will explain why. The second, however, will attempt to use the same information to move the reader to promote a specific change in New Jersey law.

What is most important about the distinction between the two approaches is the way you use facts and details about your subject. Effective persuasion relies on selecting and presenting information in such a way that your reader changes his opinion or is moved to action.

Let's go back and look at the issue of protecting our environment. Here is an opening paragraph which contains a thesis statement to persuade.

We must take action to improve our environment by utilizing our resources more wisely. This can be achieved be reducing waste, reusing items, and recycling. By reducing solid waste and transforming solid waste materials into usable resources, we can reduce air and water pollution and conserve energy.

With this introductory paragraph, the author has promised to tell us why and how we can accomplish his call to action, which is *reducing* and/or *transforming* solid waste. The introduction to a persuasive piece is extremely important because it should not only state the thesis but it should also include exactly what it is that you expect your reader to think or do at its conclusion.

Now let's practice a little. Following are ten statements ready to be developed into persuasive thesis statements. Can you identify which ones are simple statements of fact and which ones are already persuasive? Indicate with an "I" for informative and a "P" for persuasive:

_____ **1.** Capital punishment does not deter violent crime.

_____ **2.** Capital punishment should be the mandatory sentence for repeat federal offenders.

_____ **3.** Smoking should be banned in all public places.

_____ **4.** Anti-smoking advocates have accomplished smoking bans in two thirds of America's restaurants.

_____ **5.** College athletes should be paid salaries.

_____ **6.** College athletes are paid in scholarships and housing grants.

_____ **7.** State lotteries support education.

_____ **8.** Dress codes reduce truancy.

_____ **9.** Dress codes may reduce truancy, but they should not be school policy.

_____ **10.** The Greenhouse Effect should be taken more seriously.

In statement Number 1, the author will simply provide the data to demonstrate that capital punishment does not deter violent crime. It is a basic statement of fact. We can expect him/her to develop a paper with information and statistics that show there is no connection between violent crime statistics in places with capital punishment and those without. Now, if the author were intent on persuading his audience that they should contribute money to an organization that is lobbying Congress to declare capital punishment unconstitutional, he would use that same data to argue that it is important to overturn laws which do not affect the behavior they were intended to correct. The author would be using the information for the purpose of persuasion.

Now examine Number 2. The author is stating that the death sentence should be made mandatory. This is a persuasive statement and we expect him to produce the information, data, and statistics to support his argument. In writing this paper, the author would exclude the very same data that the first author chose to use. He would find information for the reverse position. Can he do that? Yes. And it is just that ability to pick and choose information that distinguishes the purely informative piece from the persuasive essay.

Now look at Number 3. If you said it was persuasive, you were correct. The statement contains the word _should_—always a sign of persuasion or argumentation. The author will likely choose information to indicate that secondhand smoke poses health risks and impinges on the rights of others.

In Number 4, we do not know how the author feels, or wants us to feel, about anti-smoking campaigns. All he promises to tell us is that anti-smoking campaigns have been successful. He or she may tell us where they've been enacted, what strategies were used, or what the result was. But the author will not indicate that he or she agrees or wants the reader to agree.

In Numbers 5 and 6 you should have noticed that Number 5 is an argument for athletes to be paid and Number 6 is a simple assertion of the fact that they earn scholarships and housing subsidies. The author of Number 6 doesn't say this is right or wrong, fair or unfair, only that it is so. The author of Number 5 clearly thinks that athletes are not treated fairly. Number 6 is factual. Number 5 is persuasive.

In Number 7 we have the beginning of a paper which will simply tell us how state lotteries support education. Does the author believe that lotteries are good? We don't know. This statement of fact could be used to bolster an argument for state lotteries and then it would contribute to general persuasion. But as it stands, it is a simple fact.

Similarly, Numbers 8 and 9 show how the statement of fact "dress codes reduce truancy" can be used to support an argument that "dress codes should not be school policy." In Number 9, the author has used a statement of fact to reinforce his persuasive statement.

By now you have some experience recognizing fact from opinion. Number 10 is an opinion—an argument that will be supported with facts taken from Greenhouse Effect literature.

Once you have decided what your opinion is and you have developed that opinion into a _should_ clause, you're ready to develop an effective introduction.

Introducing a persuasive idea or action requires that you capture a reader's interest. Your introduction becomes your *hook*. There are several ways to introduce a persuasive paper, but we'll just look at the three most common and most useful.

## A Startling Statistic

Nothing works quite so well to catch someone's interest than a simply amazing statistic. For instance, in the environmental essay, the fact that each one of us creates four pounds of garbage each and every day is enough to grab anyone's attention. Follow that statistic with the statement that the United States has an urgent need to control waste and your audience is led in exactly the direction you want them to go—to read and accept your proposal. Now, if the startling statistic is put into the words of an authority as a direct quote, it gains even more impact. For example, if we say, "According to the United States Environmental Protection Agency, each and every day, each and every American produces four pounds of garbage that must be disposed of . . . " we have added authority to our statistic.

## A Statement of Urgency

Nothing speaks better than an authority. You can grab your audience by directly quoting or paraphrasing the Surgeon General of the United States or the Secretary of the Interior. For example, "The United States Environmental Protection Agency—the people responsible for the air we breathe and the water we drink—say that unless we begin to reduce the amount of garbage we send to the landfill, the methane gas being released into the air everyday will eventually create biohazardous conditions for us all."

Quoting the EPA gives a serious tone to your introduction, and it alerts your reader that you have very important information to share which may affect their future actions.

## A Direct Question

Sometimes called a *rhetorical* question because you really do not expect an answer, the direct question invites your reader to proceed with you to discover the answer. It is your promise that if the reader goes ahead, he or she will learn. Consider this question: "How can we protect the air we breathe and the water we drink so that they don't poison our children?" This question combines a startling statement with an invitation to the reader to help find a solution.

There are other introductory devices but the above three work particularly well for persuasive writing. They establish authority, urgency, and an invitation to the reader to participate in the solution or find an answer to the question.

Let's take the development of a term paper that requires you to select a topic and argue a position. Notice, this is not just a paper about a topic, but a persuasive piece. You've got to find something controversial that has a clear pro and con and then set about writing a thesis statement to guide your research.

You brainstorm possible topics:

drug testing
animal experimentation
censorship
cheating
smoking

You decide that the idea of censorship holds some interest for you. You create a cluster map.

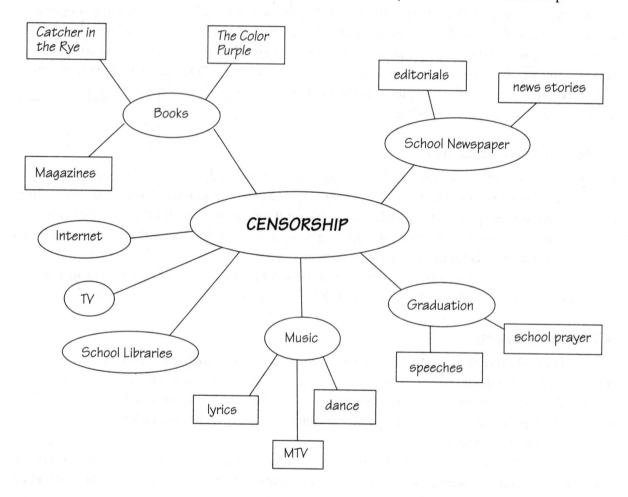

You settle on censorship in music and you weigh the two positions: should it be allowed or shouldn't it? You decide that you do not believe that any music should be censored; you believe that lyrics are free speech and listening to them is part of free expression. You establish a thesis statement to help you persuade your audience that music should not be censored.

*Censorship of music because someone or some group finds the lyrics offensive should not be allowed because free expression is a constitutional right; parents have other ways to assert control over what their children hear, and politicians should not interfere with an individual's right to choose.*

**EXPRESS YOURSELF** THESIS STATEMENTS AND EFFECTIVE RESEARCH

Is this a satisfactory introductory paragraph? It's only one sentence. It's very cut and dry. Will it make a reader want to go forward? Will it inspire a reaction either for or against? The answers to all the above are *no*. So what does it need?

*In 1985, Tipper Gore, wife of then Senator Al Gore of Tennessee, launched a campaign with Susan Baker, wife of Secretary of State James Baker, that warned parents of music's "sexually explicit language." They, and the men and women who joined them, argued that parents needed government help to raise moral children. Do we really need the government of the United States of America to use its time and resources to listen to Snoop Doggy Dog and tell us whether or not we can listen? Censorship of music—because someone or some group finds the lyrics offensive—should not be allowed because free expression is a constitutional right; parents have other ways to assert control over what their children listen to, and politicians should not interfere with an individual's right to choose.*

Notice that the thesis statement is the last sentence of the introduction. It is preceded by background information and then a rhetorical question designed to instigate thinking that the government is getting too involved in our CD collections. Would you read further? What would you expect next?

## BODY PARAGRAPHS

Now that you have engaged your reader, you must fulfill your promise. You must demonstrate with clear and convincing evidence that your thesis is correct and your reader should accept your position as his or her own. Remember the boxing strategy that was described on page ix. Let's put it to use here.

| CONSTITUTIONAL RIGHTS | PARENT OPTIONS | FREE CHOICE OPTIONS |
|---|---|---|
| 1. | 1. | 1. |
| 2. | 2. | 2. |

The box becomes a very good way to test the organization of your essay. You should always plan at least two supporting details for each argument; three or more depending on the length of the essay. The box headings are also a good way for you to check your main points. Are "constitutional rights" and "free choice options" the same? You may realize that in the struggle to find a third prong for the thesis statement that you chose too quickly and you don't have enough evidence. That's why the box becomes so helpful. As you start to identify the supporting details, evidence, and assertions under each main idea, you can revise your thesis.

## Paragraphs

Paragraphs are the building blocks of your work. Whether you are writing for information and understanding or persuasion, there are some general rules that apply.

- ➡ Every paragraph has a *topic sentence.*
- ➡ Every topic sentence must be supported with *details, evidence,* or *examples.*
- ➡ Every paragraph begins or ends with a *transition* that bridges the idea of one paragraph to the next.

One of the most common errors that students make when writing is to ignore the "mini-essay" structure of their paragraphs. If you accept that every paragraph has to have a beginning, middle, and end—just as the whole piece does—then you will be able to revise your work to assure that it is organized, logical, and clear.

Here is a sample essay. Underline the topic sentences of the paragraphs and see if you can spot the supporting evidence or examples. Identify the transition words or phrases that tie it all together.

## CENSORSHIP AND MUSIC

In 1985, Tipper Gore, then wife of Senator Al Gore of Tennessee, joined forces with Susan Baker, wife of Secretary of State James Baker, to crusade first for the censorship of what they considered sexually offensive song lyrics and then for music labeling to warn parents that it contained "sexually explicit language." They, and the men and women who joined them, argued that parents needed government help to raise moral children. Do we really need the government of the United States of America to use its time and resources to listen to Snoop Doggy Dog and tell us whether or not we can listen? Censorship of music because someone or some group finds the lyrics offensive should not be allowed because free expression is a constitutional right; parents have other ways to assert control over what their children listen to and politicians should not interfere with an individual's right to choose.

One of the first issues that must be settled before even thinking about censoring music lyrics is: is it constitutional? The First Amendment to the Constitution grants citizens the right to free speech. That has been upheld to include the written as well as the spoken word. Song lyrics are just as much printed language as newspaper editorials and just as much spoken language as recited speeches. We wouldn't even think of censoring newspapers or political speeches so why would we even consider censoring song lyrics? A rule is a rule; a constitutional protection is a constitutional protection especially when you disagree with the message.

A second argument to be made about constitutional privilege is the exception to free speech, which has been upheld by the Supreme Court. You cannot shout "fire" in a public space. You cannot use the free speech protection to incite danger for innocent people. This simply cannot apply to song lyrics. Mrs. Gore was inspired on her mission because of the Prince album, "Purple Rain," and its sexually explicit messages. She feared that hearing about certain things would promote her daughter to do certain things—but that is very different from inciting a riot. Mrs. Gore, and all the other parents out there who are worried about their children's well-being, should consider other options.

For example, rather than shifting the responsibility for protecting her child's sexual innocence to the songwriter, she could have taken more responsibility. She could have made it a point to listen to "Purple Rain" before she bought it. Then she would have been free to protect her own daughter. Another thing she could have done was to discuss teenage music with other parents. Schools are always forming parent groups. If music lyrics are a big enough threat to our young people that we're going to amend the Constitution, then what better reason to form a "Watchdogs for Lyrics" group?

This leads to a final argument against censoring music lyrics: personal choice. Shouldn't we be able to decide for ourselves what we want to listen to or read? Parents have the right to make decisions for their own children—not yours or mine. Then, once teenagers have enough disposable income that they can afford $20 for a CD, no censorship should matter; if they can earn the money they should be free to spend it. Just as songwriters should be free to write, we should be free to choose.

In conclusion, it is important that we all understand that our government has more important things to worry about than "Purple Rain." National defense, Social Security, and campaign reform are just some of the big ones. There should be no time to listen to Snoop Doggy Dog and no need. Censorship of music lyrics is unconstitutional for two reasons; there are better ways for concerned parents to fight offensive material and our personal freedom of choice must be protected.

The organizing structure behind this essay is very straightforward. It's called *order of importance,* and it uses transition words like *first, second,* and *next* to move the reader from point to point. Within the paragraphs, words such as *for example* signal the reader that evidence will follow. *In conclusion* announces the end. Did you notice that each paragraph had a main idea with supporting examples? Did you also notice that each prong of the thesis was represented as a main idea in a paragraph and then supported with details or examples? Did the essay fulfill its promise? Did it convince you that censoring music was not a good thing to do? Incidentally, Tipper Gore won a partial victory in this fight. All CDs now have warning labels which state "Contains Sexually Explicit Language." Not censorship, but a restriction.

Here is a table of transitional words and phrases that you might find helpful in planning and writing your next essay.

| ORGANIZING PRINCIPLE | TRANSITIONAL WORDS OR PHRASES |
| --- | --- |
| Order of importance | first, second, third, in addition, moreover, furthermore, more importantly |
| Chronological | then, before, as, since, later, during, when, until, while, first, second, third, next, after |
| Spatial | beside, around, beyond, under, next to, above, behind, near, along, below |
| Cause and effect | therefore, so, consequently, because, as a result |
| Comparison | likewise, similarly, just as, like |
| Contrast | on the other hand, unlike, rather, however, but, on the contrary |
| Introduce an example | for example, in other words, in fact, for instance, that is, specifically |
| Show addition | and, again, in addition, moreover, also, furthermore |
| Show emphasis | indeed, in fact, certainly |
| Acknowledge another point of view | though, granted, despite, although |

# COUNTERARGUMENTS

One of the ways that you can check whether or not you have selected a "good" persuasive topic and prepared a "strong" thesis statement is to consider if there is a strong opposing viewpoint. An argument is not an argument unless there is another side.

So, if you really want to win an argument, it is always important to anticipate what your opponents might use to *counter* your points. If you include, disprove, and dispose of them in your paper, you will have weakened the other side, not just ignored it.

Some questions for you to consider:

➡ How strong is the opposing view? Arguing against cigarette smoking is like arguing against drinking poisoned water. Everyone knows it's bad. But argue that cigarettes should not be sold to teenagers and you've got a fight.

➡ What arguments might be made against you? If you can anticipate that one of the strongest arguments against banning sales of tobacco to teens is the argument that the Constitution protects their rights, then you can effectively counter with examples of many other regulated sales such as beer.

➡ What are the weak links in your argument? If you can identify them before you write, you may be able to replace a point with a stronger one before your opposition does it for you.

This does not mean that every time you write a persuasive paper that an opposing one will be presented as well. In fact, you may be writing to an audience of one—your teacher—and he or she may know little about your topic. But every reader of a persuasive piece is also *thinking* about your arguments. A thoughtful, intelligent reader will raise questions as he goes along, then anticipate and answer them. Your paper will always be stronger.

A tip for anticipating counter arguments: prepare a chart, similar to the box below, and sketch out the *pros* and the *cons*.

Here is what a pro/con chart might look like for the Gore essay:

| PRO CENSORHIP/LABELING | CON CENSORSHIP/LABELING |
| --- | --- |
| It will protect children from sexually explicit messages. | Then we should also censor newspapers and other media. |
| The Constitution already has exceptions to "free" speech. | The constitutional exception is extremely limited and cannot apply here. |
| Parents need to be warned to help them protect their kids. | Parents need to take more self-initiated responsibility for their kids' welfare. |
| Children are already exempt from constitutional protection for their safety. | Censoring music and/or enforcing labeling hurts the rights of everyone, not just children. |

Now go back and look at the essay. Does the *con* column answer all the arguments anticipated by the *pro* side? If you read each paragraph carefully you will find that the essay does answer all the anticipated arguments.

By preparing this type of graphic organizer for your paper before you write, you are setting up your organization pattern. By composing it after you write, you can list all the points you made and then fill in the opposing viewpoints to see if you answered them. If you haven't, you can go back and revise your work to make it more convincing. The pro/con chart is, then, both a *pre-writing* and a *revision* strategy.

## SELECTING FACTS AND DETAILS

As important as it is to know how to write body paragraphs, it is just as important to know what to put into them. You've often heard arguments defined as "solid." That means that the argument is based on strong evidence, empirical data, and reliable/verifiable sources.

In other words, you're not going to argue that teenage smoking is bad because your mother said so. You're going to argue that it is an unhealthy habit because you have scientific data that proves it to be habit forming. You're not going to say that Tipper Gore should be denied her request for record labeling simply because you've heard "Purple Rain" and three of your friends found it to be perfectly clean. You'd go to the arguments founded in the Bill of Rights. Who better to support your argument than Thomas Jefferson and James Madison?

Finding the examples, facts, data, and empirical evidence to support your claim is called *research*, and the more careful you are in choosing your information, the more powerful you can make your case. It is important to comment about *plagiarism* at this point.

As you research what others have to say about your topic, you will find that someone has invariably said what you want to say better than you can ever hope to. But you cannot steal someone else's words any more than you can steal his or her money. Plagiarism is just that—stealing someone else's words or ideas, and it is a crime. In the commercial world you can be taken to court and face monetary damages. In academia you can fail a paper, even an entire course, if you've plagiarized. Be careful and responsible.

So if the purpose of research is to find out and use what others have said, how can you do that without committing a crime? The answer is by giving credit to your source of information. There are three ways to use information that you have found:

**DIRECT QUOTE:** This is when you use the exact words of someone else and set them off in quotation marks. This gives authority to your work and can be a very powerful tool. But avoid more than two or three short quotes in any 750–1,000 word paper. You don't want it to look like you couldn't think of anything to say for yourself.

**PARAPHRASE:** This is when you change someone else's words into your own but the basic idea is the same. You will do a lot of this in your writing. Research is coming up with your own argument and then finding the ideas of others to support you. The key is to make sure you "signal" your reader that while the words are yours, the idea itself is not. For example,

*According to the American Diabetes Association in its pamphlet "Living With Diabetes" there are three important ways to control this disease: diet, exercise, and medication (3).*

For signaling that you are borrowing the idea from someone else, the words "according to" become your best friend. Don't hesitate to use them. They add authority as well as honesty to your paper.

You would also have to provide an author's name and publication date on the "Works Cited" page at the end of your paper. There are two basic styles for attributing information to a source—MLA and APA. Your teacher will tell you which to use and provide a reference book to guide you. One of the best reference tools is the *Hodges' Harbrace Handbook*, published by Harcourt Brace. It contains both MLA and APA style forms and it would be a very worthwhile investment. You can also go to the websites of each: APA.org or MLA.org. Responsibly citing your sources is a very technical but very important part of the research process.

**SUMMARIZE:** This is similar to paraphrasing but you are rephrasing more than just one idea, perhaps a whole argument. You also have to "signal" your reader here as well. Again, the rules of APA or MLA must be followed.

Not only is it a legal obligation to give credit to your sources, but it also gives added credibility to your work when you quote and cite reputable and noted authorities. Take Tipper Gore: when she gathered her ammunition to fight for her belief that music lyrics could seriously harm young people, she called on respected child psychologists to provide evidence to support her claim. It was never just her word alone.

## RESEARCH AND THE INTERNET

Back in the old days, before the information explosion brought about by computers, research meant going to the library and actually gathering hard copies of books and periodicals. Today, all you have to do is log on to a search engine, and you can have more information than you dreamed possible for a given topic. How do you decide?

First, if you've done the preliminary planning we outlined above, you'll be able to limit your search to just those areas of importance for your paper. But once having done that you're still likely to find more information than you need. So how do you choose? The three words are: *current*, *reliable*, and *verifiable*.

**CURRENT:** Always check the copyright date or the currentness of the website. You don't want to use information that is outdated.

**RELIABLE:** Is the source well-known, like the American Diabetes Association, or is it Aunt Tillie's Home Guide to Diabetes Care? Does the source have a reason to be biased? You wouldn't want to rely on information provided by the "Society for Martian Welfare" to bolster your claim that we should provide more funds for extraterrestrial research. Are you working with "primary" or "secondary" material? This is a major question, especially for research on the Internet. An example would be: did you find information about the danger of methane gas from the research reported by Cornell University or did you get the information from an article that quoted the research from Cornell? The difference is important. The original research document is *primary;* the reference to the original is *secondary.* Remember, the further you get from the original, the less reliable the information.

**VERIFIABLE:** Can you find reference to the validity of the information in another reference? Has the webmaster abandoned the page? Is there a copyright symbol on the web page so you know that this is an electronic edition of a previously published text? This is important because it signals that what you've found on the Web also exists in hard copy and is likely to have been screened and juried before it was actually published. Beware the website which is no more than Wally Web's Thoughts on Pollution.

Don't fall into the trap of many inexperienced researchers—lack of adequate time. If you want to make your argument solid, you must choose carefully and selectively. You can't just grab the first piece of evidence; you have to check its currentness, reliability, and verifiability.

## CONCLUSIONS

The conclusion of the persuasive essay is just as important as the introduction. You need the *introduction* to capture your audience's interest. You need the *body* to present reasons why your call to action is important. You need your *conclusion* to leave them ready to sign up.

Conclusions should restate the thesis. You remind your audience what you promised to show them and declare that you did. If you started out with a *question,* your conclusion should answer it. If you started out with a *startling statistic,* your conclusion should return to that statistic. If you started out with a *statement of urgency* you should return to it to show why it is urgent for your audience to act.

In the sample essay about music lyrics, notice how the concluding paragraph returned to Snoop Doggy Dog and restated the thesis almost word for word. It is not necessary to repeat the thesis verbatim, but it is important to remind your audience of your original claim.

### Call to Action

Included in the conclusion of every written or spoken persuasive effort is something called the "call to action." It is your call to your audience to act on the evidence you have just presented. You want them to take some kind of action. For instance, Tipper Gore wanted Congress to pass legislation. Now that's a pretty major call to action. Sometimes the call is simply asking for a group to sign a petition or join a group or even buy a product. Sometimes the call is as simple as just thinking differently about an issue.

## PEER REVIEW

Now that you've written and revised your work, it is important to check it with an outside reader. If you really want to be sure you've written a logical, well-organized, and persuasive essay, have a friend answer the following review sheet.

## Analyzing a Persuasive Paper

Answer the questions below to see if this essay has convinced you of its argument.

**1.** What is the topic of this paper?

_____

**2.** What is the thesis statement?

_____

_____

_____

_____

**3.** What introductory strategy does the author use? Is it effective?

_____

_____

_____

_____

_____

_____

**4.** What are the three main points of the paper?

_____

_____

_____

_____

_____

**5.** What facts/statistics/expert opinions does the writer use to support his or her argument?

_____

_____

_____

_____

_____

_____

**6.** How does the writer answer the counter arguments? Is it effective?

_____

_____

_____

_____

_____

_____

**7.** Can you underline the topic sentences of each paragraph?

_____

**8.** What are the two supporting details for each topic sentence in each paragraph?

_____

_____

_____

_____

_____

_____

**9.** How does the writer conclude the paper and is it effective?

_____

_____

_____

_____

_____

**10.** Identify places where the writing is confusing or unclear. Look for abrupt transitions, gaps in arguments, or tangled sentences.

_____

_____

_____

_____

_____

While it is always helpful for a second reader to give you a careful analysis of your writing, sometimes you have to do it yourself. The rubric that follows is one widely used by teachers to grade position papers. Or, you can use the peer review sheet for your own revision. Whichever you choose, remember, there is no substitute for outside opinion.

If you would like to practice your new skills, turn to pages 147-148 for some sample persuasive topics that you can develop into a 750–1,000 word persuasive essay. Have someone peer review for you or use the rubric that follows to self-evaluate your work.

# Persuasive Essay Rubric

| | Exceptional "A" | Well Done "B" | Acceptable "C" | Attempted "D/F" |
|---|---|---|---|---|
| **Focus** | • takes a strong, well-defined position<br>• thesis is clear with 3 distinct points and 2 supporting details for each reason | • clear position<br>• 3 reasons, and some details, but not fully or well-developed | • position not clearly stated<br>• 2 reasons only<br>• few supporting details<br>• development brief<br>• unrelated, unsupported, general statements<br>• minimal facts used | • no clear position<br>• no reasons<br>• no supporting details or facts |
| **Organization** | • strong introduction<br>• clear thesis<br>• clearly developed paragraphs<br>• transitions provide logical development<br>• conclusion reasserts introduction | • introduction is good<br>• thesis is adequate<br>• paragraphs are short, not fully developed<br>• transitions are weak<br>• conclusion attempts to reassert introduction | • introduction and conclusion are present but not fully developed<br>• thesis is weak<br>• transitions are not clear | • no introduction or conclusion<br>• no thesis statement<br>• illogical organization of ideas<br>• strays off topic |
| **Use of Resources** | • demonstrates careful selection of appropriate information from a variety of sources | • information is adequate | • little use of supporting material<br>• does not meet assignment requirement | • no evidence of outside sources used |
| **Mechanics** | • error-free<br>• correct spelling, punctuation, and capitalization<br>• sentence structure is varied<br>• vocabulary is rich | • few errors<br>• some attempts at sentence variation and variety | • repetitious<br>• many errors in sentence structure and in punctuation | • errors interfere with communication of ideas |

Notice that a "C" paper satisfies the assignment but doesn't add very much in the way of selecting and using supporting information. It may have an introduction and conclusion but in general it does not demonstrate attempts to develop ideas. The "B" paper, on the other hand, would describe the Tipper Gore paper you read earlier. It had a well-developed introduction and conclusion, but the paragraphs and information were inadequate and needed further development.

In short, the "A" paper demonstrates that a lot of thought and time went into planning, researching and then revising. So, if you want that "A" you're going to have to really work for it.

# FIVE

# WRITING FOR PERSUASIVE SPEAKING

**THIS CHAPTER** will show you how to prepare for a persuasive speech. While the same rules of thesis statement, research, and supporting evidence apply, there are preparations for presentation and delivery that are unique to a speaking situation.

Many students find that when they prepare for a persuasive speech they learn techniques that help them with their writing. Unless you are asked to speak *impromptu,* the three methods of delivery you will use to deliver a formal speech are *extemporaneous, manuscript,* and *memorized.* All three of these forms require careful planning and a good bit of writing. Certainly, if you're going to read a prepared speech, it has to be written beforehand. If you're going to deliver it from memory, you have to have a text to memorize. If you're speaking extemporaneously, you have to prepare note cards to help you practice your delivery. All three types of public speaking require the same kind of careful planning, selecting, and revising that a written paper requires.

The persuasive speech, however, is unique from the written argument for three reasons. First, you will have a wider, more diverse audience in front of you. Second, you have the advantage of non-verbal communication, including visual aids, to bolster your position. Third, you will have the disadvantage of having only one opportunity to make your point; your audience cannot go back and re-read for clarity. If you don't get it right the first time, you've lost your point.

Since we have already covered the statement of purpose and thesis statement issues (see Chapter 4) let's focus on the elements of communication unique to persuasive speaking.

The structure of the persuasive speech is much the same as the written:

➡ introduce your argument
➡ argue your three main points
➡ conclude by reaffirming your thesis and presenting your call to action

## INTRODUCING YOUR ARGUMENT

The introduction of an oral presentation is also called the *interest step* because this is where you initially grab the attention of your audience. Any of the following techniques are effective oral persuasion strategies:

➡ a quotation
➡ a startling statistic
➡ an anecdote
➡ a direct or rhetorical question
➡ a statement of urgency
➡ a joke or humorous story
➡ a human interest story
➡ a visual aid
➡ a role playing invitation
➡ a personal story

Before you choose an introductory strategy you must analyze your audience. Will they "get" your joke? Nothing is worse than a joke that no one else finds funny. Will they fall asleep if you start giving off facts and figures? If it's your classmates you're addressing, you should relate specifically to them. Do they know you well enough to appreciate the importance of your personal story? It could be embarrassing if your audience focused more on you than your topic. Will your topic benefit with the use of a visual aid? If you're doing an anti-smoking piece, a picture of a diseased lung is a sure attention grabber.

A good rule of thumb to follow is that your introduction should fit your thesis and contribute to your argument and your call to action. Regardless of the introduction strategy you choose, it is your *thesis statement* that is the *most important part of your introduction*. Whatever technique you use to capture interest, it should complement and bolster your argument.

Consider the following introductions for a persuasive speech to support the need for metal detectors at school entrances.

School safety is an issue that has gained national attention in the past few years. There have been many instances of serious violence, and it is time to take no chances about the safety and well-being of our students. Metal detectors should be installed in all public school buildings because teenagers are becoming more violent; guns and knives are being brought into school buildings every day and our schools cannot be considered safe from outsiders.

Now, this is a reasonable introduction. It could certainly benefit from one of our persuasive writing introductions. But this is a speech. We want to really catch our audience's attention. So what if we were to hold up a picture of a smiling high school teenager and start this way:

I'd like you to look at this photograph of a young man who could be sitting next to you right now. His name is Adam Smith and he was one of 12 students shot and killed in his classroom at Columbine High School in Colorado by an angry classmate who decided to bring a gun to school one day. It could have happened here. A recent poll called the Metropolitan Life Survey of the American Teacher showed that 24% of students polled reported that they had been the victims of violence at school. Metal detectors should be installed in all public school buildings because teenagers are becoming more violent. Students do not feel safe at school, and we must protect ourselves from intruders.

Which introduction do you think your classmates would respond to? The second used both a visual aid and a startling statistic to introduce the thesis—*to install metal detectors in public schools*. But in this case it was probably not your thesis that captured your audience. It was the photo and the dramatic realization that a real person was actually killed in school.

## PRACTICE

Following are several thesis statements. See if you can think of at least two ways to effectively introduce each. You may wish to write out your proposal.

1. Television violence has a negative effect on society because it promotes violence, casual sex, and dysfunctional family life.
2. Elderly drivers should be required to re-apply for their driving licenses because with age comes diminished vision, hearing, and reflex action.
3. Experimentation on animals is wrong and should be stopped immediately because animals do feel pain; there are other alternatives. Experimentation is often done for cosmetics research, not for critical medical purposes.
4. Zero tolerance policies proclaim that consistency in punishment is its main objective. However, a judge recently said that "consistency should not replace common sense when handing down punishments." Zero tolerance is wrong because it punishes the guilty and the innocent arbitrarily; it creates mistrust between administrators and students; and it certainly violates a student's constitutional rights to due process.

**5.** Year-round schooling is an important innovation to consider because keeping kids in school year-round will improve their academic skills, relieve overcrowding, and provide better time for teaching certain subjects like math and foreign languages.

After you have captured your audience with your introduction, you are ready to take them through all the reasons that support your position. Like the body of your essay, the body of your speech follows a pattern which is represented in the outline below:

          I.       Introduction

Signpost

         II.      Main Point 1

             A.

             B.

Signpost

         III.     Main Point 2

             A.

             B.

Signpost

         IV.     Main Point 3

             A.

             B.

Signpost

         V.      Conclusion

It is the very same format of a good persuasive essay. You assert your introduction, then you develop the three prongs of your thesis statement with at least two supporting details for each. Then you conclude.

What are *signposts?* In a speech, the transitional words or phrases that you use to keep your audience clearly focused on your main points are called signposts. They very clearly tell your audience what point you're up to. *Signposts* in speaking are the *transitional* devices of writing. Here are some examples:

The first point I want to make is . . .

Next I want to tell you . . .

The second major reason is . . .

One of the causes was . . .

And so you can see . . .

Finally . . .

In conclusion . . .

Your signposts will depend on the organizational pattern of your speech, just as your transitions depend on the structure of your essay. In the examples above, the structure was order of importance. If you're comparing and contrasting, then you can expect to use signposts like:

On the other hand . . .
In contrast to . . .
The opposite of this is. . . .

If you're introducing an example:

For example . . .
In other words . . .
For instance . . .

Cause and effect:

Therefore . . .
Consequently . . .
As a result . . .

You can refer back to page 43 for a more complete list. Just remember, the more you rely on signposts, the more likely you are to be following the outline structure above. As a matter of fact, if you use the outline format as a template for your speech and you just plug in the words and ideas you will be sure that you are organized.

## NONVERBAL COMMUNICATION

Just when you thought you had enough to worry about with words, you find out that you have to worry about what you don't say as well. It's called body language, and it can be just as important as what you write or what you say.

### Appearance

You've heard the expression "Clothes make the man." One of the interpretations is that you can deceive people into thinking you are what you wear. Dress in a suit and tie, and you look professional. Dress in camping gear, and people will think you're a camper. Look the part—become the part.

We all know that appearance is only part of the picture. You can wear a parachute but it doesn't mean you're capable of jumping from a plane. You have to have skill and courage to match the outfit. The same is true in public speaking. You can look professional in the suit and tie, but if you have a poorly prepared speech, your clothing won't compensate for the message. But the opposite is true as well. If you have a wonderfully prepared speech and you deliver it in cut-off jeans and sandals, you may lose your audience.

Appearance tells your audience that you are prepared. It tells them that you take your subject seriously. That doesn't necessarily mean you have to wear a suit and tie, but it does mean that you are neatly groomed and clean. If you look put together you gain credibility for your topic.

## Body Language

It's called attitude. You know, the facial expression that says, "I'd rather be dead than listening to you," or the slumped shoulders which indicate total boredom. Look at some of the attitudes that are conveyed by certain physical movement:

| Openness | Insecurity | Nervousness | Frustration |
|---|---|---|---|
| Open hands | Hands in pockets | Twists note cards | Wrings hands |
| Steps in front of podium | Grips the podium | Taps or bangs the podium | Furrows brow, grimaces |
| Makes wide eye contact | Focuses on one side of the audience | No eye contact | Looks over the audience's heads |
| Smiles and engages the audience | No natural facial expression; no smiles | Giggles, laughs, breaks role | "Tsk" sound |
| Relaxed posture | Clenches mouth | Plays with hair | Short breaths |

When you are getting ready to speak to an audience, even if it's only a college interviewer, you want to remember some of these signal behaviors. You can help gain confidence and the body language that expresses it by being well-prepared.

## VISUAL AIDS

Most good speakers understand that we remember 20% of what we hear and 50% of what we hear *and* see. So it's no wonder that graphs and charts and PowerPoint presentations are a main feature of any good presentation.

For example, the speech to persuade us that we must do something about reducing, reusing, and recycling gains incredible impact with a chart that shows us what's in our trash.

# What's in Our Trash?

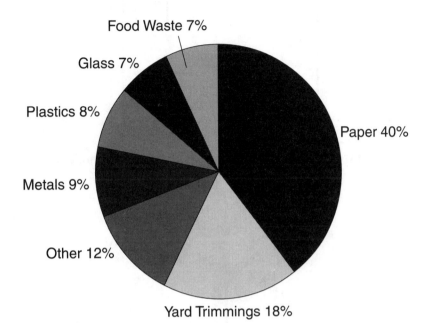

Do you see how the visual impact of the pie chart registers just how big a chunk of landfill garbage is paper waste alone?

Now imagine listening to this data being recited.

*Each person generates more than four pounds of garbage each day of his or her life. Each year, Americans receive almost four million tons of junk mail with 44% never even opened. If only 100,000 people stopped their junk mail, we could save up to 150,000 trees annually. If a million people did this, we could save up to a million and a half trees. Americans also throw away the equivalent of 30 million trees in newsprint each year. And when you consider that 85% of our garbage is sent to the landfill—where it can take from 100–400 years for things to decompose—you realize that we are leaving our children a lot of garbage!*

Think how much easier it would be to understand all those numbers if you could only see some of them in relation to what they meant. What if the speaker used the following graphics to display the highlights of his data as he spoke?

The average family receives 4,000,000 tons of junk mail each year!

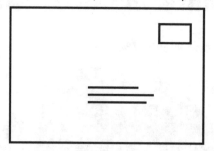

150,000 trees could be saved if only 100,000 Americans stopped their junk mail.

It can take 100–400 years for 85% of our garbage to decompose.

Recycling newspapers for one year could save four trees.

**EXPRESS YOURSELF** WRITING FOR PERSUASIVE SPEAKING

Looking for an effective conclusion, the speaker might want to remind his audience of the main point of his persuasion which was to promote reducing, reusing, and recycling waste. His conclusion would also be aimed at telling his audience what they might do to vitalize the effort. So rather than rely on words alone, he prepared this graphic to display as he concluded:

---

**REDUCE**

- BUY GOODS IN BULK. IT TAKES MORE MATERIAL TO PACKAGE PRODUCTS IN SMALL QUANTITIES.
- READ MAGAZINES AND NEWSPAPERS ONLINE.

---

**REUSE**

- INSTEAD OF PLASTIC UTENSILS OR PAPER PLATES, USE THE REAL THING.
- DONATE CLOTHES, TOYS, AND OTHER DISPOSABLES TO THE NEEDY INSTEAD OF THROWING THEM AWAY.
- BRING YOUR OWN CLOTH SACKS TO THE GROCERY STORE INSTEAD OF USING PLASTIC BAGS.

---

**RECYCLE**

- ALWAYS BUY PRODUCTS MADE FROM RECYCLED MATERIALS SUCH AS PAPER TOWELS, GARBAGE BAGS, GREETING CARDS, AND STATIONERY.
- PARTICIPATE IN COMMUNITY RECYCLING BY SORTING CANS, BOTTLES, AND OTHER WASTE.

---

## Other Types of Visual Aids

Today's technology makes it incredibly easy to produce colorful transparencies or PowerPoint slides. But even if you don't have the advantage of the overhead projector or computer projection capabilities, you can still use:

- poster boards
- models
- flip charts
- photographs
- costumes
- demonstrations
- samples
- video clips
- handouts

Whatever visual aid you use, you are only limited by your creativity and the following important guidelines:

1. Limit transparencies or other aids. You want them to have impact so save them for the most important points. A common rule is one visual for each two minutes of speaking time.
2. Emphasize the visual impact. Use more graphics and fewer words.
3. Use at least 20-point font for text.
4. Use only 3–5 colors in a visual aid.
5. Do not read directly from your visuals; use them to supplement your speaking.

We remember 20% of what we hear and 50% of what we hear and see.

## THE COLLEGE APPLICATION AND VISUAL AIDS

It's no accident that many college applications request a photo. Imagine how much easier it is to read a form with lots of data and have a face to which to attach it all. And if you're an athlete you already know that your prospective coaches want to see a video; if you're an artist, it's your portfolio; if you're a dancer or a musician, it's the demo tape. But what if you're just plain old you, no fancy videos to share? Well, consider this. You, too, can have a portfolio!

Once you've been called to an admissions interview, plan to bring a portfolio of your most outstanding efforts with you. Have a series of photos of you cheerleading, clips from the school newspaper that you edited, or certificates of accomplishment that you've earned. A simple 5–8 page binder with your name and photo on the cover, that includes samples of your work with photos for support, can be just the creative edge you need to separate you from the other applicants.

The same thing applies when you go for that summer job you need or the competitive internship. Whatever you do to distinguish yourself from the pack will work to your advantage. Remember, you're only trying to be persuasive, and people recall 20% of what they hear and 50% of what they hear and see. So give them something to look at!

Speaking of college applications, let's move on to the next chapter, which is all about how persuasive writing impacts your everyday life, and certainly, persuading someone that you should be admitted to their school is right up there in importance.

# SIX

# PERSUASION IN EVERYDAY WRITING

**THIS CHAPTER** explains some of the everyday

purposes for persuasive writing. You will learn

how to apply some of the skills you have just

learned to write: letters of complaint, letters to

the editor, and college application essays.

Just like writing for information and understanding, writing to persuade is used in everyday life. Whether you're trying to persuade a store to refund your money, or want the editor of your school newspaper to accept your position on an issue of importance, you must follow the basic guidelines of effective persuasion:

➡ **Understand your purpose.** Know exactly what you want before you start to write. Do not sit down to write a letter of complaint about a product that you have purchased unless you know exactly what it is that you expect to happen as a result of your letter. For example, do you want a replacement? Do you want a refund? If you start writing before you know, chances are your reader will never get to the request before dismissing your letter as just a nuisance.

- ➡ **Know your audience.** Remember back in Chapter 3 of section one when we talked about tone? The same rules apply here. Your level of formality, your choice of words, and your sentence structure will be determined in large degree by your audience.
- ➡ **Make your position or request clear in the first paragraph.** If you're clear on what you want to happen, you should make that known immediately. Then you can go on to explain why it would be important for your reader to fulfill your request.
- ➡ **Support and develop your position or request with reasons, evidence, and examples.** The amount and kind of support will depend on the task. A letter of complaint would not include pages of information, but a cover letter asking for an interview might need more development.
- ➡ **Organization is always important.** When you want something specific to occur, you want to be sure you have presented a logical and coherent piece of writing. In a persuasive piece of writing such as the letter of complaint or the cover letter requesting an interview, your first paragraph should establish what you want and why the reader should go on reading. Each paragraph should then develop the reasons why and conclude with a restatement of your request.
- ➡ **Grammar counts!** A letter of request, whether high stakes like the job interview or the college application, or low stakes like the letter to the editor, requires attention to the conventions of standard written English. Nothing is worse than distracting your reader with the wrong "its" or the wrong "you're." Misspellings stand out like you've spilled coffee on the page! Run-ons or comma splices confuse your reader and distract his or her attention from your message. So make sure you have a second reader.

## THE LETTER OF COMPLAINT

Let's look at some practical examples. You have just purchased a brand new clock radio/DVD/telephone combination. The clerk in the store said it was guaranteed for one full year. You got it home and the DVD player doesn't work. What's worse is, the phone won't ring if the radio is playing! Something is obviously wrong. You go back to the store and the clerk says, "No problem. But I can't help you here. Once you buy it and it leaves the store you have to write to the manufacturer." Let's see how you do.

1. Exactly what do you want? Do you want a replacement? Do you want to get rid of the thing forever? Do you want it fixed? You must decide before you start writing and you should know what your warranty says. You don't want to demand a replacement unless that's an option. So you decide that if you have a one-year warranty you are going to ask for a replacement. You don't want this one "fixed." It's brand new and shouldn't need repairs. Besides, you don't want to take the chance that it will break again.

2. You write to the manufacturer. Rest assured, the president of Sony or Aiwa won't read your letter. It's going to be one of many customer relations associates, and they follow company guidelines. Because you have read your warranty carefully before you sat down to write, you know that your request is doable. If you present yourself as knowledgeable and confident, rather than nasty and demanding, you have a much better chance of having your request answered. Threats and demands have no place here.

3. Be specific and factual. The first sentence of your letter will include the specifics of what the item is, where it was purchased, when it was purchased, and what is wrong. Leave nothing out. The second sentence will state the problem. The third sentence will state what you want to happen. The rest of your letter, one or two more paragraphs, will include the facts to support your request—when the radio is on, the phone doesn't ring, and so on.

4. You've written your letter and you check it for misspellings and homonym errors, but you decide to let your mother take a look at it. What do you think she'll say?

---

100 Customer Road
Electronic City, TX
June 15, 2001

Clock Heaven Radios
200 Digital Drive
Circuit, CA

Dear Customer Service,

I bought this clock radio at one of your stores back in March. I've had nothing but problems with it. I hate it and I wish I'd never bought it. You state that I have a one-year warranty; I sure hope you'll honor it because I want this thing fixed or I want another one. I'd really just like my money back so I can buy another brand altogether because yours is really no good.

If I don't hear from you in ten days I'll have to write again and maybe even call my lawyer!

Thanks,

Joe Customer

---

Your mom reads this letter and suggests several changes. Your revised version looks like this:

---

100 Customer Road
Electronic City, TX
June 15, 2001

Clock Heaven Radios
200 Digital Drive
Circuit, CA

Dear Customer Service,

On March 14, 2001 I purchased a Clock Heaven Radio/DVD/Telephone system from Consumer World. I have experienced three problems with the machine. The phone does not ring when the radio is on. The DVD player does not work. The clock falls behind every day. Your product came with a full one-year warranty, and I would like to have a replacement system.

Because there are so many major faults with the system I have, I do not want it repaired. I want a replacement. Please let me know where to return the system and pick up a new one. Consumer World has said that I must deal directly with you so please let me know if I should send the system back to you or if you will authorize Consumer World to take it back and give me a new one.

I appreciate your help with this. Clock Heaven Radios has a great reputation and I would certainly like to add my satisfaction to the list of happy consumers who own one.

Sincerely,

Joe Customer

---

There is a world of difference between the two letters. Notice the conclusion of the second letter. It appeals to the company's sense of pride and customer satisfaction. It assumes that the company wants to be helpful; this is very unlike the first letter, which assumes that the company needs to be threatened with a lawyer.

But don't be misled. Even though the second letter is clearly more proficient, it is not necessarily written by a professor of college English with a gift for writing. It is basic and factual, with a specific request that has an appropriate sense of audience and tone.

You should be able to write that kind of letter. All it takes is a little time to be thoughtful and careful.

## THE COVER LETTER: APPLYING FOR A JOB

One of the most important letters that you will ever write will be the letter requesting a job interview. But make no mistake, at its core it is simply another piece of persuasive writing and the same rules apply. This time, however, you want to:

- address the letter to a specific person
- include in the first paragraph the specific job for which you are applying
- present your qualification
- suggest why you are uniquely qualified
- request an interview and be specific about when you are available

In this letter, the object of your persuasion is the interview. It is always best to write to a person, rather than a title. For example, find out the name of the person who is hiring. Rather than address your letter, "Dear Head Counselor," try to find out the name of the head counselor and use it.

In your first paragraph, state where you read or heard about the job, what the exact job is, and summarize your qualifications. Much like the thesis statement, this summary of qualifications serves as the organizing principle for the rest of the letter. Let's practice:

You're looking for a counseling job at a summer camp. Your aunt heard that Happy Acres is looking for an arts and crafts counselor, and she found out that the Head Counselor is James Smith. You decide to apply. Happy Acres is a great camp and you really want the experience. Using proper headings, the body of your letter would look like this:

---

Dear Mr. Smith,

I have heard that Happy Acres Camp is looking for counselors for the upcoming 2002 camp season. I have previous experience as a camper and I have worked all this past year in an after school program for junior high school students. I enjoy working with kids and I am creative and reliable.

I was a camper at Green Acres Day Camp for three years and remember how much I enjoyed Arts and Crafts. I still have the pencil holder I made with popsicle sticks. I used some of my experiences as a camper when I started working in the after school program at my local junior high school. I was told by my supervisor that my arts and crafts projects were some of the most creative that he had seen. One in particular was enjoyed by the kids. We made photo frames from braided leather and many of my kids used them as Christmas gifts because they were so good.

I never missed a day of work and I could always be counted on to help with any extra work that was needed. I'm sure that my experience, creativity and reliability will make me a good counselor for Happy Acres.

I would like to meet with you for an interview and I could see you any day after three o'clock. I look forward to hearing from you.

Sincerely,

Connie Counselor

---

Did you notice that:

- The letter was written to a specific person.
- The first paragraph stated the job being applied for.
- The first paragraph gave a general statement of qualifications and interest.
- The second and third paragraphs developed the qualifications with specific examples.
- The last sentence asked for an interview with times of availability.

Try going into the classified ads and finding a job for which you would like to apply. Follow the format and see how well you do.

## THE COLLEGE APPLICATION LETTER

Persuading the college of your dreams that you should be admitted is perhaps the biggest writing challenge you have yet to face. So much depends on it and you want it to be right. Most colleges require that you submit a writing sample to judge your qualifications and some of the samples ask for very creative efforts. We'll discuss later the "narrative of personal experience" which is the foundation of most college application essays, but for this chapter let's assume that your college has simply asked you to complete an application and part of it is a brief essay.

The essay prompt might look like this:

> *Please write a brief explanation as to why you have chosen Maryville College for your undergraduate work.*

It will probably be followed by lines, which are intended to keep your response limited to the space provided. *Never* start writing on the application itself. Wait until you've gone through the whole process of prewriting, rough drafting, revising, and editing before you fill in the application.

Like the cover letter, the college application is looking for information about you and you must be very clever to use the limited space provided to present the best of yourself. One of the first things you want to do is read the college catalog. Look for the school's "mission statement" or an explanation of its heritage and philosophy. Try to extract a phrase or sentence that you can use to connect to the school. For example, in the Maryville College catalog (Maryville College is in Maryville, Tennessee and it is ranked as one of the best small liberal arts colleges in the South) the following goal is stated, "to educate students to see beyond personal interests to their roles as citizens." How can you use this? Consider the impact of beginning your response this way:

> *I have chosen Maryville College to be my home for the next four years because I have always believed that personal interest should be second to my role as a productive citizen, and I believe that Maryville's philosophy of education will help me realize my potential.*

Do you see how the language from the catalog has helped you bridge the connection between yourself and the school? Of course, you have to go on to develop this connection with specific examples. You will also want to construct other bridges between yourself and the school as you go along and the more specific information that you have the better. However, the introduction to this brief essay has set the path for you. You could go on as follows:

> *I have read the catalog carefully and believe that the opportunities for study abroad, public service internships, and the college's emphasis on environmental issues will help me to develop my personal goals and interests. I have been active as a volunteer for our local homeless shelter, and I worked each year in high school on our school's Earth Day projects. Last year I was Chairman of Earth Day 2001, and we worked to bring attention to the increasing air pollution in our national parks. Maryville is very close to the Great Smoky Mountain National Park, and its Mountain Challenge program is very interesting to me. I believe that I can contribute enthusiasm, energy, and commitment to Maryville.*

If one paragraph is all you have space for, and it often is, then the paragraph above demonstrates how to say a lot in a little space. Notice something very important. This student has carefully examined the college catalog and really knows why Maryville is a good choice. No college recruiter wants to think that you know little or nothing about the school. They are looking for a four-year commitment, and the more you know about them, the more likely that you'll make a contribution to the school and complete your four years. To summarize:

➡ Know the school well. Include specifics about the school's philosophy or its programs to anchor your interest to the school itself.

➡ Offer specific examples about yourself to demonstrate that you have experiences in which the school will be interested. Remember, you want them, but they have to know there's something you have that *they* want.

➡ Watch your grammar and mechanics. This is another place where you don't want to be dismissed because you don't know "there" from "their."

Now it's time to look at narrative writing and the college essay.

# WRITING TO NARRATE

**NARRATIVE WRITING** is telling a story in order to establish an idea or assert an opinion. It follows all the conventions of good storytelling such as characterization, plot, and theme, and it is often used as a means to get you to write about yourself. Narrative writing is sometimes called reflective writing.

Narrative writing is often thought of as creative writing because it is assumed that if you are going to write a story it is going to be just like a story written by an established author. But this is not always the case. As a matter of fact, narration is frequently used to add interest or emphasis to informational or persuasive writing.

Remember the anecdote or personal story used to begin a powerful persuasive essay or speech? That is also a form of narrative writing.

For our purposes in this section we will look at three ways that narrative writing can be used.

➡ narratives of personal experience
➡ narratives for academic purposes
➡ narratives in everyday life

In the first chapter, we will explore the various ways that you are asked to use your personal experiences to write about yourself. From the "getting to know you" essay that you are asked to write on the first day of every English class to that college application essay, personal narratives are an integral part of your school writing experiences.

In the second chapter, we will look at ways that a good story can enrich and invigorate even your most basic content-area reading and writing. From science to social studies, putting factual information into story form can be a very powerful study tool.

In the third chapter, we will look at narratives in everyday writing such as journals, diaries, letters, and even e-mails.

But before we begin, we must look at the general characteristics of narrative writing which include:

➡ characterization
➡ plot
➡ setting
➡ theme

All good stories have lively, memorable *characters*. By creating such characters, the writer invites the reader to participate in the experiences of the character(s).

The experiences are the *plot*, which is the sequence of events that the characters go through in order to establish the meaning or significance of the events.

The significance of the events—what they mean, and what the characters have learned from them—is called the *theme*.

Where all this occurs—the place, the time, the weather—is called the *setting*.

Read the following narrative of personal experience, written by a high school senior reflecting on a very important turning point in his life. See if you can identify the characters, the plot, the setting, and the theme, as well as the literary elements that contribute to good storytelling—figurative language (similes and metaphors), foreshadowing, irony, allusion, and even symbolism.

## HEARTBREAK

Heartbreak. One of the most important lessons that I will have learned in high school is heartbreak. Despite all the teachers impressing upon me lesson after lesson of how to write, how to solve equations, and even how to speak another language, I will always remember my lesson in heartbreak.

At Farragut High School, the privilege of attending Prom remains the highlight of most students' junior year. After two years of hard work, students graduate to the status of an upperclassman. Consequently, they receive the right to attend Prom, of course after paying a nominal fee, as nothing in life comes free of charge. To this end, I encountered heartbreak with no exception, as it proved costly both physically and emotionally.

Sunday, two months before prom, I finally mustered up the courage to ask a girl, whom we shall call H.B., short for heartbreak. In asking her, I followed the philosophy, "If you are going to go, go all out!" The look of shock on H.B.'s face when I appeared at her door that fateful Sunday afternoon reassured me that I had broken all expectations of how a guy should ask a girl to the Prom in an original manner. I felt I had nothing to worry about when H.B. said she needed to think about her answer. Girls always took time to answer. Didn't they? Such is the way of life. As I rode home, I imagined ways that H.B. would answer my question, always expecting the answer to be, "Yes."

Later that night, after eating dinner, the telephone rang. As my mother shouted up the stairs that H.B. was calling, my heart jumped.

I recalled all the effort that led up to asking H.B. to the Prom. I mused over the various dates bowling with friends, the Winter Dance, and the movies. I called to mind the occasions in which I bought roses for no reason in particular. I thought back to the occasions in which I emptied my wallet to brighten her day. I recollected coloring the words "H.B. will you go to the prom with me" on the six-foot-long by five-foot-high banner. I remembered attaching all twenty-four red and white helium filled balloons. I reminisced in the memory of attempting to fit the "float" into my mom's van and then attempting to walk inconspicuously to H.B.'s front door. I saw again the look on her face as she opened her door. However, this time her face appeared not happily surprised but painfully shocked.

At that moment, everything, all my efforts, all my emotions, all my expectations that lay balanced on the scale of life suddenly became weightless in comparison to the heavy words that landed on the other end of the scale. "I am already going to the Prom with someone else."

My heart came crashing to earth like Wile E. Coyote after another failed attempt at catching the roadrunner. Indeed, the Acme fabric wings disintegrated, the Acme helicopter fell apart, the Acme jet-powered skates ran out of fuel, unraveled and snapped all at the same time. Acme must have also made my Prom expectations because at that moment, they too disintegrated, fell apart, ran out of fuel, unraveled and snapped altogether. I expected a wonderful evening with a girl for whom I cared. I expected to continue building a relationship with H.B. I expected that my expectations would transform into reality. Most important of all, I expected her to say, "Yes."

In short, I realized none of my Prom expectations. My relationship with H.B. also ended abruptly. A simple, "Yes" became an even simpler, "No." My Prom plans and my relationship plans became simpler still. H.B. had picked me to the bones like desert buzzards with a newfound carcass and it will take a long time for it all to heal. Heartbreak.

1. Can you identify the theme? What is the author telling us about heartbreak?
2. Are the characters memorable? Do you have an image of the author and H.B.?
3. Is the plot clear? Do you notice how the story unfolds with a distinct beginning (pre-Prom), middle (asking and then waiting for an answer), and end (heartbreak)?
4. How about the setting? Can you picture the "float"? H.B.'s front door?

5. Did you recognize any literary devices? The reference to Wile E. Coyote is called "allusion." Being picked to the bones "like desert buzzards" is a simile. "My heart came crashing to the earth" is personification. "That fateful Sunday" is foreshadowing. And there were two other instances of foreshadowing. Can you find them?

6. How about the excellent visual details (imagery) used to describe the "float"?

All in all, this was a very successful narrative of personal experience. Now let's see how all of this can be applied to other narrative situations.

# SEVEN

# NARRATIVES OF PERSONAL EXPERIENCE

**THE NARRATIVE** of personal experience allows you to communicate to your reader the people, places, and events in your life that have been of significant influence. What you choose to write about and how you present the information and emotions indicate a great deal about your values and attitudes.

Doesn't it seem that every time you walk into an English class, the teacher asks you to write something about yourself? Your teacher is just trying to get to know you and to know something about how "well" you can write. The "well" part means how well you handle the conventions of standard written English like sentence structure and usage. The "getting to know you part" is how creative and insightful you are.

Some of these "getting to know you" assignments aren't very good ones. They give you little help in figuring out just what to write about. But most English teachers know that to get a good product they have to give you some good directions and helpful pre-writing conversation. When it comes to the narrative of personal experience, the key to the writing is in the pre-writing.

Consider this assignment given on the first day of school and due tomorrow:

> *We have all had experiences that have changed the direction of our lives. These experiences may be momentous or they may be experiences that did not loom so large at the time, yet they changed our lives forever. Recall such a turning point in your life and present it so that you give the reader a sense of what your life was like before the event and how it changed after the event.*

After you get over the original feelings that (1) nothing momentous ever happened to you and (2) what you feel was momentous you could never write about in your English class, you're going to have to come up with something. Where do you even begin?

## PRE-WRITING STRATEGIES

For most narratives of personal experience, the cluster map or lists which center from the five *w*'s is always a good place to start. Remember, you're writing a story, so the *who*, the *what*, the *when*, the *where*, and the *why* are all potential topics. Start by identifying:

**WHO** (relationships that are/were important)

| | |
|---|---|
| Kristy, my best friend | My grandmother |
| Mother | Sister |
| Boyfriend | |

**WHAT** (things that are important to me)

| | |
|---|---|
| My grandmother's locket | My diary |
| My old sneakers that my mother wants to throw away | My "Stage Right!" trophy |
| My pillow | |

**WHEN** (times I remember most)

| | |
|---|---|
| Camp "Stage Right!" the first day | The beach last summer |
| When my grandmother died in the hospital | When my mom and I had a huge fight |

**WHERE** (places that are or were important)

| | |
|---|---|
| Camp "Stage Right!" | My grandmother's kitchen |
| The beach at Mary's summerhouse | My bedroom |

**WHY** (reasons to remember who, what, when, where)

| | |
|---|---|
| Camp "Stage Right!" saved me from being a total recluse/nerd! | My grandmother was so special I still miss her. |
| My mother and I always fight and I hate it so I go to my room. | I loved my drama coach. She made me feel special. |
| I think I can write about camp "Stage Right!" because that's where I loved being the most. | It changed my life forever and even my mother started coming around after that summer. |

Notice that by walking slowly through the five *w*'s, you began to find "focus." You began to isolate the times and places most important to you. When you got to "why" you began to define the reasons for the importance, and you began to realize the focus of your writing.

### CHANGING NIGHTMARES INTO DREAMS

Imagine the typical sixth grade nightmare. Remember the first year of middle school. Think about expectations versus realities and the sense of utter confusion that enveloped you as an awkward sixth grader just about to enter seventh grade. Remember the strange feelings of insecurity, shyness, and no confidence. Well, I remember.

I was the epitome of the lost twelve-year-old. I was lost in life with no direction and no purpose. I had frizzy red hair and typical teenage skin problems, a closet full of ugly neon clothes, and a rude, introverted, "cool" attitude. I appeared extremely shy and unmotivated.

Then, the summer after sixth grade, my friend Kristy invited me to go to "Stage Right!" with her. "Stage Right!" was a camp sponsored by the Knoxville Performing Arts Institute. At this camp children were taught singing, dancing, and acting, and they learned how to make stage props and costumes. I thought it sounded like fun, but little did I know that camp would influence me to audition for the group that would change my life forever. That group, Kids Unlimited, gave me self-confidence, personality, and performance skills, and I learned to love life and strive to be my best.

This was the first rough draft of the introduction to a narrative written in response to the assignment above. Before we go on with the rest, let's look at these three paragraphs. Do you see the thesis statement? Remember, that's the sentence(s) which tells the reader what the piece is going to be about. Even narratives have thesis statements, especially when they are being written to answer such a direct question prompt. Do you see that it's buried in paragraph three? The thesis, when we finally get to it, is *That group, Kids Unlimited, gave me self-confidence, personality, and performance skills, and I learned to love life and strive to be my best.*

Does that mean that all the rest is no good? Not at all. It simply means that a little revision is necessary. Camp "Stage Right!" started out as the main topic, but once the writer began to write it became clear that it was Kids Unlimited that was the true focus of this piece. The first two paragraphs are warming us up for Kids Unlimited but they can be shortened and made much more dramatic. After re-reading, the writer decided to change the introduction with a much more direct invitation to the reader:

Remember when you were a shy, awkward sixth grader, uncertain of anything and everything you said and did? Remember when you hated how you looked and just wanted to disappear? Well, I was the epitome of the twelve-year-old lost in life with no direction, no purpose, and no talent. I had frizzy red hair, typical teenage skin problems, a closet full of ugly neon clothes, and no self-confidence at all. My life was a nightmare until "Kids Unlimited" unleashed my personality, gave me confidence in myself, taught me how to love life, and strive to be the best I could be.

The author kept the excellent description of "frizzy red hair," but took us more directly into the heart of the piece. Now watch where she decided to go next.

But before "Kids Unlimited" there was "Stage Right!"—a summer camp for young teens that helped us to learn to act, sing, dance, plus make stage props, and costumes. I went to "Stage Right!" because it sounded better than staying home in my room all summer, and it was the best decision I ever made. I made friends and discovered that I enjoyed things I never even knew existed—like singing and dancing on stage. I had so much fun and felt so much better about myself that I didn't want that summer to end. So I auditioned and was accepted for "Kids Unlimited," a traveling troupe of young performers.

From the very beginning, everyone at "Kids Unlimited" worked together for a common purpose. We wanted to learn and to perform. We learned the importance of stage presence, which gave me poise when I walked and talked. We sang and danced constantly, and I found that I had a natural gift for music. I was often complimented on my hard work, which gave me confidence and pride. But the best part was traveling to new places and meeting new people.

I traveled extensively with "Kids Unlimited." We performed on a cruise ship in the Bahamas and a cruise ship to Mexico. We took a performance tour of New York City, Niagara Falls, and Toronto, Canada. We sang at the White House, the Kennedy Center, the Hard Rock Café, and anywhere else that wanted to see 22 kids singing and dancing in sequin bow ties. I was confident because I had great friends and personal poise, not to mention the fact that I could entertain a crowd and love every minute of it. Being in "Kids Unlimited" was an experience that truly changed my life.

Let's go back to remembering that awful sixth grader. I remember that time when I disliked myself and did not think I would ever enjoy life. When I was selected for Kids Unlimited I learned the forms of expression that I needed in order to be confident and personable. I became a great performer with a drive that has never left me—a will to be my best and the confidence to change nightmares into dreams.

Go back and look at the assignment. Does the author fulfill the purpose, which was to tell about a time in her life that changed things? Does she make it clear what life was like before and then after? Do you get a sense of just who the writer is? The answer to all three questions is "yes." But what makes this piece truly special is the vivid description of "frizzy red hair, teenage skin problems, a closet full of ugly neon clothes" and the conclusion which is so dramatically tied to the introduction.

**EXPRESS YOURSELF** NARRATIVES OF PERSONAL EXPERIENCE

## More Pre-Writing

While lists and cluster maps are always a good place to start, there are other pre-writing strategies that inspire good writing about personal experience. Often, these warm-up techniques are part of the assignment itself. Consider the following prompts, all topics taken from a variety of high school and college introduction essays.

1. Consider the following quotation: "It is better to have loved and lost than never to have loved at all." Write about a time in your life when you learned what that quotation meant. It does not need to be romantic love that you write about. It could mean platonic love or a familial relationship.
2. React to the following bumper sticker by telling about a time in your life when it proved true: Animals are man's best friends.
3. Movies and books often talk about the importance of loyalty and friendship. Tell about a time in your life when friendship proved to be of great importance to you.
4. Martin Luther King Jr. said that he wished for the day when his children "would be judged not by the color of their skin but by the content of their character." Tell about a time in your life when the content of your character was tested.
5. The way a person handles disappointment tells a great deal about what is important to him or her. Tell about a time in your life when you confronted disappointment and learned from it.

You will notice that the prompts themselves provide the direction that you must take in deciding what to write about. Each one provides the "theme" for your story. Remember that "theme" is the main idea you will be discussing. To answer the first question, you will be writing about your feelings concerning love. You will have to think about a time in your life that tells why you either agree or disagree with the statement.

To answer the second question, your theme is your opinion about animals. Do you agree that they are worthy friends? To answer the third question, your theme is loyalty and friendship. Can you think of a time in your life that proved the statement true or false? The fourth question's theme is character. Were you ever forced into a situation where you had to demonstrate honor, loyalty, or trust? The theme of the fifth question is the effects of disappointment. Can you think of a time when disappointment caused you to understand yourself or others?

Once you have identified what your topic is and you have figured out a time in your life that illustrates your point of view, you can begin to write. Remember, you are writing about a specific time so you want to determine the parameters of the experience. When did it begin? How long did it last? How and when was it resolved? In other words, you need to narrow your experience to a set period of time.

Then consider who the people were who contributed to your experience. They become your characters. Be certain to limit the number of people to just two or three, because in a three- or four-page essay you want to focus on the experience and not distract your reader with too many players.

Then establish the time and place—the where and when of your story. This is your setting. All that is left is your plot. The how and why your characters interacted enables you to come to the conclusions you did about your topic.

Sounds easy? Well it should be. You're being asked to write about the things that are the most personal to you and about which you have all the information you need. Let's see how one student responded to the second topic.

Mary decided that the second topic was perfect for her because she has a dog at home that she has raised since puppyhood. She knows firsthand how much she loves Tasha and what a good friend she has been whenever Mary felt lonely or just needed a companion to take for a walk. But that's not really what the topic is asking for. It specifically said, "Tell about a time when the statement proved true." So Mary must isolate a specific time, place, and experience that she shared with Tasha that showed her that Tasha was truly her best friend.

Mary jotted down all the memories of Tasha that came to her mind:

Frisbee in the park
Sleeping at the foot of her bed
Waiting for her at the bus stop
Keeping her company whenever she was sick

But none of these little things seemed enough to write an entire essay about. And then Mary remembered Belle, a golden retriever she and Tasha met at the park one Sunday. Belle was an assistance dog, and she was with her owner who was in a wheelchair. It was a beautiful Sunday and the dog, Belle, was chasing a ball that the man in the wheelchair was throwing. Mary had her story:

### A DOG NAMED BELLE

Many Sunday mornings I take my dog Tasha for a run in the park. She's trapped in the house most days and she loves to run free and chase her Frisbee, so I try to take her to the park at least once a week. I usually see my friends there, but one Sunday I met a man named Patrick who was throwing a ball for his dog Belle. Nothing unusual about that except that Patrick was in a wheelchair, and while Belle and Tasha chased their toys I had a chance to talk to Patrick. I learned far more about Belle than I did about him. This is the story of Belle and how I know for sure that animals are man's best friends.

Belle was a four-year-old golden retriever when she was dropped off at the local animal shelter. She had been a Christmas puppy—one of those cute doggies that grow up and people decide they don't want anymore. She was going to be destroyed because no one really wanted to adopt a four-year-old dog. The animal shelter tried adopting her but she was shy and not very outgoing. Three families had brought her back because she just wasn't what they wanted.

And then the local shelter offered her to the Canine Assistance Program of Alpharetta, Georgia, and Belle found her calling. She was trained to be an assistance dog. She learned how to respond to over 100 commands and Patrick told me how she picked up things he dropped, opened the refrigerator door for him, helped him off with his coat, and hundreds of other chores that he can't do for himself.

When he called Belle over for a formal introduction, I could see the absolute love she had for her master. She rested her head in his lap and when her ball fell to the ground she snatched it up and dropped in right back in his lap because she knew that he couldn't bend over to reach it. She had the gentlest eyes, and the way Patrick stroked her head, I could tell that he loved her as much as she loved him.

He told me that before Belle came into his life he was often very lonely. He didn't come to the park on Sundays because he had no reason to go to all the effort it took to get his wheelchair in the van. But with Belle, the park was worth the trouble because it made her so happy. It also gave him people to talk to. Before Belle, people avoided him. With Belle by his side, he made new friends every day.

We talked for almost two hours that Sunday in the park. We all became friends. Many Sundays when I take Tasha for her weekly outing I see Patrick, and we always have a lot to talk about. Tasha and Belle play and I have learned that animals truly are man's best friends.

Does this essay fulfill the assignment? Check it against the rubric.

| EXCELLENT | • fulfills the requirements of the prompt |
| --- | --- |
| | • has a definite sense of time, place, characters, and theme |
| | • creates an insightful and memorable experience |
| VERY GOOD | • fulfills the requirements of the prompt |
| | • time, place, and characters are adequately developed |
| | • experience is adequately developed |
| GOOD | • fulfills the requirements of the prompt |
| | • time and place shift and the characters are thinly presented |
| | • experience is trivial and not fully developed |
| | • repeats words and phrases |
| WEAK | • minimally fulfills the prompt |
| | • time and place is vague and characters are not developed |
| | • experience is flat and poorly developed |
| POOR | • barely satisfies the assignment |
| | • is not limited to one experience and does not develop time, place, characters, and theme |

# THE COLLEGE APPLICATION ESSAY

At a time when competition for college acceptance is fierce indeed, the college essay may be one of the most important parts of your application. Once candidates have been narrowed down by high school rank, grade point averages, SAT scores, and extracurricular activities, it is often the essay that provides the tiebreaker. Writing about yourself, commonly referred to as "The Narrative of Personal Experience," is a powerful way to distinguish yourself from others.

The narrative of personal experience provides many opportunities for you to convey to others what events, people, or activities have helped to shape your character and goals in life. The essay requires careful planning because you are often limited to 500 words. The essay about Belle is approximately 500 words long so that should give you an idea of length. However, the essay about Belle is lacking some critical information if it were to be used as a college application essay. First, it does not make reference to anything the author has learned about herself. Second, it does not translate the experience into any hint about interests or goals for the future.

Let's see how the Belle essay might have been written for a college essay. The prompt might have been:

Briefly describe why you believe that you can contribute to the academic community at Anywhere College.

I discovered one Sunday morning not too long ago that I wanted very much to help those who were either disabled or otherwise unable to fully participate in life's daily activities. That was the Sunday morning I met an assistance dog named Belle and learned the story of how these remarkable animals were trained to be helpmates to people who needed them.

Belle's story convinced me that service to others is the greatest service that an individual can contribute to his or her community. I know that Anywhere College recognizes the importance of service, and I hope to participate in the college's Habitat for Humanity Program and its overseas outreach service courses as I pursue a major in Social Science.

I know that the next four years will teach me much, and because my life's goals came into focus with the chance meeting with a wonderful dog, I am open to experiences and ideas. I would welcome the opportunity to participate at Anywhere College and receive the guidance and support that the school can offer.

This brief response (200 words) uses the Belle experience to construct a very focused and personal response to a section on an application that provided only a small space. But what will distinguish it from others is that it is specific to the school and unique to the individual.

The "Common Application," which many schools accept, requires a lengthier essay. The application itself was designed so that students didn't have to recreate their personal information a dozen or more times on many different application forms. It also saved colleges and universities from having to create hundreds of different writing prompts.

So let's see if you can let Belle once again be helpful. Use both the sample responses above and revise them into one 500–750-word essay that responds to the following prompt. Or you may practice this essay type using any personal experience that you may have.

We are interested in learning more about you and your personal and academic goals. Please tell us about your interests and goals. Describe a time in your life that illustrates who you are and what you hope your college experience can provide for you.

Possible topics to consider:

camping experiences

sports or team experiences

community service projects

school clubs (music, art, business)

participation in government projects

travel experiences

exchange student experiences

family crises

health issues

childcare experiences

church/synagogue/mosque activities

It is never too early to start planning your essay of personal experience. Think about the places, people, and events that are meaningful to you. Start keeping a journal or diary to record them.

Remember that whenever you read the words, "Tell about a time . . . " You are being asked to write a narrative of personal experience.

## TIPS ON WRITING ABOUT PERSONAL EXPERIENCES

Every time you are asked to write something about yourself, you don't have to start from scratch. Following is a list of resources that you carry with you wherever you go, right in your memory. If you want to begin keeping track of some of these experiences, try jotting them down in a journal. The best writers use bits and pieces of their everyday lives to enrich their writing.

**Teachers:** What have your teachers taught you—in class or from their lives? Start by making a list of your teachers' names, and see what stories that list brings to mind.

**Family Generations:** Who are the older people in your life, and what stories do they tell? Do you remember your grandmother? How about younger siblings?

**Friends:** What can you learn from friends? Their stories are part of your repertoire.

**Family Stories:** What family stories or activities give you special insight? Common stories within the family may amaze outsiders.

**Be a Professional Eavesdropper:** Take dictation from the world. What can you write in your journal from what you overhear on the bus, in the hall, on the road? What have strangers taught you?

**Dreams:** Keep a notebook and record your dreams.

**Places:** What places in your life give you a special way of seeing and feeling?

**Thoughts:** What are your thoughts about the news, the state of your school, the future, the present? Trust your own experiences, thoughts, and feelings. Treat yourself very seriously, and you'll be surprised how others will react. Everything has the potential to become a good story.

# EIGHT

# NARRATIVES FOR ACADEMIC PURPOSES

**USING STORIES** to relate information and/or recreate historical events are a rich literary tradition. Whether you use the power of narration to help you study or you use it to present your own analysis of information, it is an important writing tool.

## HISTORICAL FICTION

Have you ever sat in a social studies class and dreaded the recitation of facts and details about people, places, and events that had absolutely no connection to you or your life? Did you find it incredibly difficult to find a way to remember who was who, and where and when all of the information came together? Unfortunately, too few history books recreate history with a true sense of narrative purpose, which is, simply put, a good story. Now this is not to say that there is no place for history books. The *chronological recording of significant events, which are accurate,* is what history is all about. But sometimes adding a good story makes it all memorable. In fact, the first definition for history in Webster's New Collegiate Dictionary is *tale* or *story*.

However, the stories told in history, science, or sociology are obliged to be factually accurate. Non-fiction, by definition, means true. But there is nothing like a good story to keep us interested and bolster our memories. That is why *historical fiction* is such a popular literary genre. The term itself seems a contradiction. If history is true then how can it be fiction? Well, historical fiction means that the events, places, dates, even some of the characters are likely to be factually accurate, but that the stories are not necessarily true. Consider the novel by Stephen Crane, *The Red Badge of Courage*. It takes place during the Civil War, and its main character is a young boy who is fighting. The data about the war, details such as the types of weapons, the number of wounded, the kinds of injuries, the lack of supplies, and the harsh camp conditions are all factually accurate. But they become the conditions and experiences of a young man, like any teenager, who must deal with them. The young man is a made-up hero and his character's feelings and fears are the author's speculation. Does that make the story not historical? No. It makes it memorable.

Few students who have read *The Red Badge of Courage* forget that the Civil War took place in America from 1861–1865—not because they memorized that information, but because they remember the main character—a boy fighting for his home. The details surrounding his extraordinary story became part of the story itself.

Other notable books of historical fiction include:

*Johnny Tremain* by Esther Forbes: a young boy's story of life and fighting in the American Revolution.

*The Good Earth* by Pearl S. Buck: a peasant family's life and struggles in China in the early twentieth century.

*From Here to Eternity* by James Jones: interwoven stories about soldiers and military life in World War II.

*Better Times than These* by Winston Groome: interwoven stories about soldiers and military life during the war in Vietnam.

*City of Darkness, City of Light* by Marge Piercy: interwoven stories about the women and men of the French Revolution.

*Tale of Two Cities* by Charles Dickens: juxtaposed life in France and England during the French Revolution.

*Stones from the River* by Ursula Hegi: the life and times of a German village during World War II.

*Dream of the Walled City* by Lisa Huang Fleischman: about China and a young girl's friendship with Mao Zedong.

*The Dress Lodger* by Sheri Holman: England during the cholera epidemic of 1831 provides an accurate account of life in nineteenth-century England.

*My Antonia* by Willa Cather: a young girl lives on the prairie during the nineteenth century.

*Giants in the Earth* by O.E. Rolvaag: the story of Norwegian settlers in the northern United States during the 19th century.

*Girl With A Pearl Earring* by Tracy Chevalier: the story of a housemaid in the home of the Dutch painter Vermeer in the late 17th century.

**EXPRESS YOURSELF** NARRATIVES FOR ACADEMIC PURPOSES

When you are studying a period or a place in history, ask for a good story to help you connect to the times and places. There are hundreds that your school librarian can suggest. The stories will help you understand and remember because they will provide a rich human face to the fact and details of your study.

But how does all this relate to the writing that you can do? Well, one very important way to study history is to create your own stories around the information that you are expected to know. For example, just as you study World War I, and have a hard time remembering just when it occurred and why it happened and who some of the principal figures were, years from now students will study the attack on the World Trade Center. They will be challenged to learn the details of that awful day, September 11, 2001, when New York City and Washington, D.C. were attacked. Right now, we probably couldn't find an American who couldn't relate every detail about the horrors that occurred. But twenty years from now, when this awful assault on our country is part of our history and not part of our present experience, one way that students can learn it all is to read or tell a detailed story. Consider how this brief fictional narrative integrates important factual data while at the same time creates a very real human drama.

Tuesday, September 11, 2001 dawned a bright day. Gina Kovak prepared breakfast as usual and watched her firefighter husband, David, help their two young daughters get their shoes and socks on as they got ready for the school bus. The girls, ages five and seven, hugged their dad as he waved them off to school, promising them a trip to Burger King when he came home that evening.

Gina got David's coffee mug ready to go, and at 8:05 A.M. he began his commute from their Perth Amboy, New Jersey home to his firehouse in Manhattan's business district. David kissed Gina goodbye and she began her daily chores. At 8:55 she turned on the TV to keep her company as she folded laundry and heard the first news of what everyone thought was an accident but quickly learned was a terrorist attack on the World Trade Center.

Her immediate thoughts were shock and horror, but she didn't really worry about David. Then she watched a second plane slice into the second tower of the World Trade Center. Then she heard and saw the explosion at the Pentagon. Then the plane in Pennsylvania crashed. Then she began to worry about David.

The day was long and filled with worry. She couldn't reach him, but she knew that his firehouse would have been one of the first to reach the scene. She also knew that when the first tower collapsed and then the second that David was certainly right in the heart of it. She carried a stone in her heart all day, a sick feeling that nothing relieved. She watched the reports on television of the terror unfolding at the Pentagon where they feared that hundreds had died. She learned that passengers on the Pennsylvania flight had actually thwarted their hijackers and brought their plane to the ground to save civilians on the ground. By the evening of September 11, 2001, Gina knew that Dave would never come home.

He became one of almost 3,000 Americans destroyed by terrorists. He became one of many fathers who would never see their babies in Halloween costumes that year or ever. She would have to face Christmas morning alone with her little girls, and every Christmas morning from now on.

Who did this and why? Gina asked herself that question over and over. Terrorists who hate the United States—that was the answer that the politicians gave. Osama bin Laden was named as the mastermind, a man who hid in the faraway country of Afghanistan. They hate us because we love freedom and peace, Gina thought. They hate us. Gina couldn't understand how anyone could hate Dave.

September 11, 2001 was the day that the United States of America declared war on terrorism and began a long period of military and diplomatic actions. September 11, 2001 was the day that began the rest of Gina's life without her best friend and husband.

Now, evaluate the narrative using the following rubric.

| | FOCUS | CONTENT | STYLE | MECHANICS |
|---|---|---|---|---|
| **EXCELLENT** | • insightful approach to the topic<br>• clear understanding of the narrative task<br>• 5 *w*'s are established | • accurate details<br>• well-developed<br>• creatively integrated into text<br>• point of view is clear | • creative use of character, theme, and tone<br>• excellent sentence variety<br>• excellent use of vocabulary<br>• use of dialogue | • error-free or minimum errors that do not interfere with communication |
| **VERY GOOD** | • topic is clear<br>• understanding of the narrative task is clear<br>• 5 *w*'s are established | • accurate details used to develop the topic and point of view | • character, theme, and tone are clear<br>• some sentence variety and vocabulary choice | • minimum errors |
| **GOOD** | • topic is clear<br>• understanding of the narrative task is faulty<br>• 5 *w*'s weak | • some accurate details not always well-developed or logically distributed | • character, theme, and tone are uncertain<br>• little sentence variety<br>• simple but accurate vocabulary | • errors that cause confusion |
| **WEAK** | • topic is uncertain<br>• poor or no understanding of the narrative task<br>• No sense of 5 *w*'s | • inaccurate or vague use of details<br>• poor development not logically connected | • character, theme, and tone are confused<br>• poor sentence structure and poor vocabulary use | • mechanics interfere with communication |

**EXPRESS YOURSELF** NARRATIVES FOR ACADEMIC PURPOSES

You may now consider transcribing your social studies notes into stories to help you remember details. After you have written your story, go back to the rubric and see how well you did. Here are some sample activities to get you started:

1. Write an account of a day in the life of a Confederate soldier after the Battle of Antietam. Be sure to include details about his food, uniform, and spirit. Include dates and important battle sites and names of generals.

2. Write up your notes about President Truman's dilemma to bomb Japan to end World War II as if you were the President writing in his diary. Be sure to include two reasons why he was sure he was right and two reasons why he thought he might be wrong. Include dates and names of famous people who were part of Truman's cabinet.

3. Become a spectator at President John F. Kennedy's funeral procession and relate the sights, sounds, and conversations you hear. Be sure to talk about the speculations surrounding his assassination and include reference to the vice president who succeeded him.

4. Recreate a day in the life of a child working in a factory in Great Britain during the Industrial Revolution. Be sure to include details of his entire day, from rising in the morning to going to bed at night. Give dates as a reference, include the name of a specific city, and name a specific item of manufacture.

5. Describe the farm life of a Chinese peasant. Include details of his housing, farming tools, crops, and general working and living conditions. Include location and even the names of Chinese officials.

Even though you might not be assigned these writing topics, you should still consider making them part of your independent study program. You could also ask your teacher for help in identifying what a good narrative prompt would be. Often, students complain that they just don't understand something and they simply give up, when all the while they have the tools at their disposal to make new ideas meaningful to them. Writing stories is one such learning tool. Try these:

➡ A day in the life of . . .
➡ A diary entry for an historical figure
➡ Recount an historical event from the perspective of a citizen
➡ Write a letter from one historical figure to another

You will find that if you write this way and force yourself to use the details of dates, times, places, names, and numbers, you will look up important information and use it. This becomes reinforcement for your learning. Memorizing in isolation is never as effective as using information for a purpose. What better purpose than telling a good story?

## HISTORICAL NON-FICTION

The concept of learning about history through a fictionalized yet factual story is similar to learning about history through a completely accurate story. Historical writing that uses only verified and accepted historical evidence can be as compelling as its fictional counterpart. Biographies and autobiographies are just two examples. Like the non-fiction described above, these stories are rich human dramas told as good stories about people, places, and events that actually happened. Consider the very popular autobiography *Angela's Ashes* by Frank McCourt. His story of his childhood in poverty-stricken Ireland has given his readers remarkable insight into the anger and hostilities between Northern and Southern Ireland and between Ireland and England.

Similarly, the very carefully researched biographies written by Carolly Erickson, such as *Bloody Mary*, the life of Mary Tudor who ruled England in the mid-sixteenth century, give remarkably accurate pictures of the life and times she writes about.

Whether you rely on non-fiction or fiction, good stories are the heart and soul of history. They will serve you well to read and write them.

## NARRATIVES FOR SCIENCE

Do you remember that wonderful science fiction book-turned-movie called *Fantastic Voyage*? More people learned more about the circulatory system and the organs of the body from the movie than any science or health class could ever hope to teach. In case you don't know the film or the book, *Fantastic Voyage* was the story of a miniaturized ship that took scientists through the bloodstream of a sedated patient. Sure it was science fiction, but it presented accurate visuals and vocabulary about the body. You might want to rent the film, it's a classic.

Like the historical fiction we listed here, some science fiction that is based on accurately developed scientific evidence include the medical thrillers of Michael Crichton and Robin Cook. Both men are scientists and use their knowledge of practical and theoretical science to provide the background for some fascinating stories. Ask your librarian for help locating their work. You'll be surprised how exciting it will be to learn science.

Apply the same rule of storytelling to help you learn science concepts. By writing out the information, you help to identify what you don't know so you can look it up and apply it. For example, create a story about how the periodic table was developed. You can do a little research to help you gather information and then write a brief paragraph about why the symbol for gold turned out to be **Au.** You'll find that memorizing the symbols will become easier because you will have a pattern for your learning.

Anything you study becomes easier when you write about it. Writing is thinking. By putting your thinking on paper you can identify what you don't know or what you are confused about. You can then look up information or re-read for clarification. If you attempt to write a narrative you always start with the 5 *w*'s, so right off the bat you have to identify key information.

# NINE

# NARRATIVES IN EVERYDAY LIFE

**EVERYDAY LIFE** provides another set of stories

for each of us. As we become more dependent

on our computers to communicate with our fam-

ilies and friends, we become more and more

reliant on our ability to tell a good story. Whether

it's a letter, a note, or a simple e-mail, if you

present a good story you've turned simple com-

munication into a welcome correspondence.

There's nothing like opening a letter or e-mail from a friend or relative, especially if they live far away and your communication is primarily electronic. Many people also find that it takes less time to use the computer than it does to use the phone. You don't have to plan time during a busy day because you can compose your letter any time, day or night, without waking anybody up. Without the back and forth of conversation you can say what you want and sign off for later. But that doesn't mean that your correspondence should be devoid of careful planning and editing. One thing that the new generation of computer correspondents has learned is that computer composing follows the same rules as pen and paper.

# E-MAIL

E-mail has changed the face of business communication. We can send the same message to dozens of people with one keystroke. But there are rules that apply to e-mail in the workplace, and it is never too early to learn them. Wherever you work you will find computers available, and you must be very cautious when using them.

Ohio State University Professor Kitty O. Locker defines a person who follows the etiquette of computer communication as a *netizen* or a citizen of the world of computers. It is a very important definition. Just as citizens of a country must abide by the laws of its land, so must the citizen of cyberspace abide by its rules. Some of those rules are unwritten and are only now being defined. For instance, criminal behavior in cyberspace, like unleashing a virus on innocent and unsuspecting users, can be punished through the legal system. But you are more concerned with the unwritten rules of etiquette. Here are just a few:

➡ Never use all capital or all lowercase letters.
➡ Always follow the conventions of standard written English.
➡ Don't use code or abbreviation.
➡ Avoid forwarding chain letters and junk mail.
➡ Do not use profanity.
➡ Organize your message as if you were writing in longhand.
➡ Create subject lines that are clear, concise, and correct.
➡ If you use your business computer for personal correspondence, it is *not* private.

You may have noticed that there seems to be little difference between this list and a list that might be written for regular writing. In fact, what separates e-mail in business from personal e-mail correspondence, is the very specific nature of the business writing and the fact that it is not private. If you use your business computer for personal use, many people, including your employer, will have the right and opportunity to read it. Consequently, you should always use the computer at work with the same care that you would if you were handing in a paper or mailing a letter with your signature on it.

That being said, what about your home computer? Nobody has access to it, so who cares about the rules of etiquette? Not true. Just as you practice good manners at home to ensure that you'll likely be well-mannered outside, practicing good writing all the time makes you more confident and skilled when you most need it. Your friends deserve to see and read good writing, and you should take the opportunity to develop your skills. You can't practice enough!

Three important qualities of computer-generated writing apply to any writing that you do. They are voice, tone, and style.

You may remember that back in Section 1, Chapter 3, we talked about attitude and tone. Well, another way to describe attitude is *voice*. Your writing should always have your signature voice in it, and you never want to convey a poor or negative attitude. But you may want to convey a mood or a tone. Perhaps you are sad or angry or just plain happy. Word choice and the use of literary devices such as similes, metaphors, and personification, go a long way to developing an exciting and entertaining correspondence. Let's start with word choice.

## CONNOTATION AND DENOTATION

You've heard the words *denotation* and *connotation* before. Denotation refers to the dictionary definition—it's a very literal use of the word. Connotation means word choice to convey *more* than its literal definition. It means using words to imply meaning or even exaggerate meaning. Take for example the verb "to cry." Very literally it means to shed tears as in, "The boy cried when he lost his mother." But if we say that the boy "sobbed" when he lost his mother, look at how much more information we have conveyed. Do you think the boy who cried was as upset as the boy who sobbed?

Choosing words deliberately and thinking about what they imply as well as what they mean can help you give life to your writing and story telling. Look at these verbs and see how many others you can think of which mean the same but have stronger meanings.

Cry

Run

Talk

Love

Laugh

Enjoy

Eat

Sleep

Walk

Sail

Write

Now let's see how some of these verbs and their synonyms were incorporated into an e-mail from one friend to another.

To:         Mary
From:      Jane
Subject:   Disneyland Adventure

I just thought I'd take a minute from dashing from ride to ride to let you know how things are going here. We are having a blast. We haven't stopped wolfing down the corn dogs and cokes, and when we fall into bed at night we are so exhausted that we enter dreamland in seconds.

My brother sobbed his little heart out yesterday when he didn't meet the height requirements for the roller coaster, and my mom could barely console him. He has been having a great time, and he races to each activity with unmatched energy. I can't keep up with him.

Yesterday was spectacular for me. I went sailing with friends of my dad's. I never knew that wind and sun and water could be so exhilarating. As tired as I was when we got back, I felt as if I could have gone on forever. I just adored the whole experience.

Gotta run. I'll write more later.

Can you isolate out the verbs in this brief e-mail that gave it so much energy? First, dashing from ride to ride rather than simply running; wolfing down corn dogs not just eating; entering dreamland instead of sleeping; sobbing and not just crying; races instead of runs; exhilarating instead of fun; adored instead of liked.

## FIGURATIVE LANGUAGE

Another way to enliven your writing and your storytelling is to create effective similes and metaphors. Remember those? Similes are comparisons which use *like* or *as* and metaphors are comparisons that change one thing into another without using like or as.

Here are some examples:

Simile: He was as tall as a skyscraper.
Metaphor: He was a skyscraper compared to the other kids.

Simile: My dorm room feels like a prison.
Metaphor: My dorm room is a prison.

Simile: Her face was as bright as sunshine.
Metaphor: Her face brightened the room with its light.

Metaphors accomplish many things for your writing. They demonstrate your creativity. They invite your reader to use his or her imagination. They allow you to say in a few words what it might normally take you many words to say. Remember the image of "picked clean by desert buzzards" to describe the feeling of being rejected by a girlfriend. Need we say more about how awful the young man felt?

See if you can come up with similes and metaphors for these:

Your room
Your English teacher

Your car
Your biology textbook
Math
The prom
The yearbook
Christmas
Jell-O™
Your pet

## SENSORY DETAILS

Like similes and metaphors, sensory details invite your reader to participate with your writing. By incorporating the five senses into your images, similes, and metaphors, you connect your personal experiences and insights to the physical world shared by us all. Most effective description relies on verbs, adverbs, and adjectives. Consider these:

My dog is white and tan, small and very lively.
A whirlwind of white and tan fur, my dog loves to run.

Alexandra was a little girl who smiled and laughed and loved to hear the sound of her own voice.
A sunshine smile as broad as her face, a laugh that matched a symphony, little Alexandra charmed
    everyone at the family reunion.

The car sounded as if the car battery was dead.
The engine struggled to turn over and gasped and gasped before it finally was silent.

Now try to use the similes and metaphors you created above, add sensory details or rewrite them completely using only sensory details. Try to use touch, taste and smell, as well as sight and sound. Can you provide sensory details to describe the following?

Your room
Your English teacher
Your car
Your biology textbook
Math
The prom
The yearbook
Christmas
Jell-O™
Your pet

It's fun and challenging to create these images and comparisons without necessarily planning a big piece of writing. If you start thinking this way and keep track of interesting images as you go along, you may find that you have a collection to choose from when you need them. You may want to keep a journal or diary to record your daily thoughts and activities.

## JOURNALS AND DIARIES

Perhaps the most personal of personal writing is the diary. You know—the one that has a lock and key that nobody is allowed to read? If you don't have one, and it doesn't have to be locked, you should start one. Just jot down your thoughts and images as they occur. Keep a written record of things you find amusing or sad, things that make you angry or happy. You might even record scraps of conversation that you overhear. You'll be surprised when you actually use some of the things you've observed to invigorate a stale and boring piece of writing.

You can also use a journal or diary to record lengthy reactions to your daily experiences. Many people start writing daily snippets and snatches and then find themselves recording entire pages of detailed narration about their daily experiences. Not only do these recordings serve as reference tools for future writing, they also provide a rich personal history for you to examine and re-examine as you grow and change.

Writing also helps you to fully explore the events and emotions of your everyday life. When you least understand yourself or your friends or family, writing about them can bring focus. Similarly, when you least understand your feelings, writing about them can give them visibility, and it's always easier to deal with a friend or an enemy that you can see and touch.

And that brings us back to where we started. Remember page 1? Writing gives visibility to your thinking. Whether you write essays for information and understanding, for persuasion or for personal introspection, writing makes your thinking visible to the world.

Express yourself!

# WRITING IN RESPONSE TO LITERATURE

Reading and responding to a piece of literature requires much the same approach as reading and writing to demonstrate information and understanding about social studies, social science, or other subject-specific content. However, there are some elements to organizing and then analyzing and evaluating literature that are unique. This section will prepare you for some of those special concerns.

**J**ust when you think you've begun to understand the dynamics of tackling almost any writing situation, up pops another. Writing in response to literature is a category of its own. It requires specific skill in certain areas. For instance, there are four main genres in literature and each has a set of characteristics that contribute to its meaning.

This section will take you through three of the four genres:

➡ poetry
➡ prose (fiction)
➡ drama

The fourth genre, prose (non-fiction), was explained in the discussion of reading and writing for information and understanding in Chapter 1.

You will explore how responding to a poem or a short story goes way beyond "I liked it" or "I hated it" to a much more focused and precise analysis of:

➡ plot
➡ character
➡ setting
➡ theme

This section will have three chapters. Each chapter will explain how to write about one of the three major genres and how to analyze the elements of literature stated above: plot, setting, character, and theme.

Chapter 10 will cover how to read and examine *poetry* for meaning and message. Chapter 11 will concentrate on *short stories* and show you how to read more deeply into a text for its implied meanings and then how to craft short essay responses and develop supporting evidence. Chapter 12 will do the same for *drama.*

# TEN

# Writing About Poetry

**THIS CHAPTER** will explain some of the unique

characteristics of poetry and show you that it's

probably easier to read and write about poetry

than you thought. Tips for understanding theme

and then using the language of the poem to help

you craft a response will be demonstrated.

You are probably just like thousands of others who hear the word "poetry" and respond by saying either, "I don't like it," or "I never could understand it." It is true that poetry is more complicated than other forms of literature, and it takes more skill and patience to penetrate. Because poems compress major ideas into few words and rely on figurative language (metaphors and similes), you are often left on your own to analyze and interpret possible meaning. You can never expect to fully understand or quickly appreciate a poem's significance in only one reading.

For example, let's take a look at the following poem by Emily Dickinson, regarded as one of America's greatest poets. Her style is unique. No two poems are alike, and there are no rules to help you figure out what she is saying. She writes about the biggest of subjects—death, life, love, and nature—in the smallest of ways. Her poems are short explosions of thoughts and feelings. Look at the poem below:

*We play at Paste—*
*Till qualified, for Pearl—*
*Then drop the Paste—*
*And deem ourself a fool—*

*The shapes—though—were similar—*
*And our new hands—*
*Learned Gem—Tactics*
*Practicing Sands—*

Emily Dickinson didn't title her work. This puts the reader at a disadvantage because unlike more traditional poems the reader has no signal about the subject. Instead, there is an invitation to the reader to bring his or her own insights to the poem and even declare his or her own subject. To analyze a poem this way, there are certain questions that you should bring to any reading of poetry, and we will use them to analyze the Dickinson poem.

1.  What is the subject of the poem? She uses the pronoun *we* which is a clear indication that she is writing about something common to us all. She writes about *Paste*. Is she talking about children at play? She says we *play* until *qualified*. Does she mean we start out *playing* until we are ready for more serious, *qualified*, work? The second stanza refers to *new hands* and mentions that we *practice* until we *learn*. A very literal interpretation of the poem could be that the poet is telling us that the play we engage in as children prepares us for more serious, skilled work as adults. But this is just the surface meaning. We have to go beyond and explore the figurative world of the poet's words.
2.  Are there any metaphors or similes in the poem? Remember that metaphors and similes are the comparison devices that writers, not just poets, use to convey deeper meanings. By comparing their thoughts and feelings to common things and common experiences they help the reader connect to the poem. So what could Dickinson mean by *playing at Paste*? Why would we feel *foolish* to learn something new? What could we learn that would turn our ability into *gem tactics* and not just *playing* or *practicing* in the sandbox like children? What are the *similar shapes* she is talking about?

Re-read the poem and see if you can construct some meaning to the piece that goes into some of the "bigger" issues of daily life. What could the poet be comparing child's play to? Could this poem be talking about love? About life itself? How could life and love apply to playing in sand?

The metaphor that Dickinson is using in the poem compares the adult's understanding of life and love as being a *gem*, in contrast to the child's preparation to understand life and love as being *sand* or *play*. She tells us that we only play at living and loving until we are ready to appreciate the magnitude and importance of it all, and only then do we see how foolish we were to take it all for granted. And only then do we realize that what we have and what we are, is gem quality—true and real. It is the difference between real diamonds and fake glass—the difference between real pearls and paste copies.

**EXPRESS YOURSELF** Writing About Poetry

When she writes that the shapes were similar she means that early love may look and feel like the "real thing," the gem, but it really isn't; it's just an imitation. Ultimately, she is telling us that we prepare our entire lives for understanding the *gem* quality of our lives and relationships. Until that moment when we reach understanding, we are merely *playing*.

Are you now sitting back and saying, "I would never have thought about all that myself?" The answer is no, not if you're used to reading quickly and with little thought. Poetry, like all good literature, requires careful, thoughtful reading if you're going to have something intelligent to say about it. Now look at the study guide questions that follow. They relate to the poem we have just worked with. See if you can write responses to the questions.

**1.** What title would you give this poem? Explain.

_____

_____

_____

_____

_____

**2.** What is the metaphor on which the poem is based?

_____

_____

_____

_____

_____

**3.** What line, phrase, or word has the most meaning for you? Why?

_____

_____

_____

_____

_____

**4.** With whom would you share this poem? Why?

_____

_____

_____

_____

_____

Let's look at possible responses.

**1.** I would call this poem "Child's Play" because it really is about the importance of child's play. The author tells us that everything we do, even the silly games we play, is preparation for the most important lessons in life.

or

I would call this poem "The Jewelry of Life" because the author compares costume jewelry with real jewelry to tell us that we have to learn the difference in order to ever have any gems of our own. She is really saying that everybody can have real pearls if they just look hard enough.

**2.** The metaphor in the poem is comparing children at play to adults. By comparing children to adults the poet tells us that unless we learn important lessons we will never have real love or a real appreciation for life and like children we will always be playing.

or

The metaphor in the poem is comparing real jewels like pearls to costume jewelry made up of sand. Sand becomes pearls after years in the ocean. The author is comparing the process of sand becoming a real pearl. To the reader, it symbolizes being really alive after spending years playing at relationships and taking life for granted.

**3.** I like the line ". . . Gem tactics" because it says exactly what the poem is about. We need gem tactics to really get the most and the best out of our lives and relationships. The word "tactics" means that love does not happen automatically, but we can learn how to make it happen.

or

I like "till qualified for Pearl" because it tells me that I may not be ready yet to be really in love. I may not be qualified. To be qualified I need more practice and just like my little sister, I am still learning by using all my friends and family.

**4.** I would share this poem with my boyfriend. He thinks he is in love with me but I know that he's just "practicing." I want him to be my "pearl" but I know I am not his even though he says so.

or

I would share this poem with my mom because I know that she has learned the difference between fake jewelry and real. I know that she understands real love and does not just say it. And then I would share it with my sister who has a boyfriend who keeps telling her he loves her, but he really doesn't. He isn't "qualified" yet because he's still playing and my sister is going to get hurt.

Having prepared answers to these questions that forced you to think about the literal and implied meaning of the poem, you are ready to write a more comprehensive analysis. See if you can respond to the following question:

Emily Dickinson's poem "We Play at Paste" is a small verse packed with big meaning. Write a 500-word explanation of the poem being sure to consider the poet's use of language and figurative detail.

_____

_____

_____

_____

_____

_____

_____

_____

_____

_____

_____

_____

_____

_____

_____

_____

_____

_____

_____

_____

_____

_____

Now let's examine two poems by a contemporary of Dickinson's. Like her, Walt Whitman is considered one of America's foremost poets. Read his poem below:

A NOISELESS PATIENT SPIDER

*A noiseless patient spider,*
*I marked where on a little promontory it stood isolated,*
*Marked how to explore the vacant vast surrounding,*
*It launched forth filament, filament, filament out of itself,*
*Ever unreeling them, ever tirelessly speeding them.*

*And you O my soul where you stand,*
*Surrounded, detached, in measureless oceans of space,*
*Ceaselessly musing, venturing throwing, seeking, the spheres to connect them,*
*Till the bridge you will need to be formed, till the ductile anchor hold,*
*Till the gossamer thread you fling catch somewhere, O my soul.*

Is this poem really about a spider? On a literal level it certainly does talk about a spider. It describes how the spider sits in isolation and spins a web by throwing thin filaments trying to connect one to the other to build a foundation for itself. The spider tries to connect, to find a place. And he does this hour upon hour, almost endlessly. And he is patient.

But then in line 6 the poet shifts to himself and Whitman begins comparing himself to that busy, patient spider. He says that like the spider, he too keeps throwing out attempts to connect himself to the world. He tries to make connections and he calls those connections *bridges*. We learn from studying about Walt Whitman that, like Emily Dickinson, his bridges to the world were his words, his poems. When we read his poem "Full of Life Now," he makes it quite clear that his verse is the way he asserts himself.

**EXPRESS YOURSELF** WRITING ABOUT POETRY

FULL OF LIFE NOW

*Full of life now, compact, visible,*

*I, forty years old the eighty-third year of the states,*

*To one a century hence or any number of centuries hence.*

*To you yet unborn these, seeking you.*

*When you read these I that was visible am become invisible,*

*Now it is you, compact, visible, realizing my poems, seeking me.*

*Fancying how happy you were if I could be with you and become your comrade;*

*Be it as if I were with you. (Be not too certain but I am now with you.)*

Can you find the place where he tells us what year he is writing in? Can you find the line which tells us how old he is? Can you find the line(s) which defines how he has constructed his bridge to the future? What words does he use to let us know that unlike the spider his connection is tangible and permanent?

Like the Dickinson poem, you have to think beyond the poem itself. You have to read between the lines and look for the comparisons. What is Whitman using of his to compare to the filaments that the spider throws? If you substitute poetry (words) then you see that as the spider struggles to connect to the world so does the man who wants his soul to be realized. Like the spider's filaments, the poet uses words. At the age of forty in 1884, Walt Whitman has defined his soul and connected it solidly to the present and the future, forever, with his words and his poems. His connections are solid, visible. He goes so far as to say in the last line that if you are reading his verse then indeed he is very much with you right now!

Try answering these questions:

**1.** What is the metaphor on which "A Noiseless Patient Spider" is based?

_____

_____

_____

_____

_____

**2.** What does Whitman mean when he refers to his Soul in both of these poems?

_____

_____

_____

_____

_____

**3.** What does Whitman think about the power of poetry in "Full of Life Now"?

_____

_____

_____

_____

_____

**4.** What is the line(s) in either of the poems which have the most meaning for you? Explain.

_____

_____

_____

_____

_____

Here are some sample responses:

1. Walt Whitman is comparing himself to a spider. He says that like the spider, he tries to connect himself to the world by throwing out a web; however, his web is made up of his attempts at relationships, his efforts to connect to the world and create his place.

2. When Whitman refers to his Soul—always with a capital letter—he means that his soul is his essence. He wants to have his soul known to many so that his life will have meaning and connection to others.

3. Whitman thinks that his poetry is very powerful. He says that even though he is "invisible" his poems make him "visible" and "compact" through his reader. In other words he can be seen and even touched through his poetry. His poetry also makes him immortal because he tells us that he is 40 and the year is 1883 because he wants us to know that when we read his poem he is still right here.

4. My favorite line is "realizing my poems, seeking me . . . " This is the heart of the poem. Whitman is telling us that his poems, when "realized" or read and understood, are evidence that he is still of the world. His poems have made him immortal.

## COMPARISON/CONTRAST

Often you will be asked to compare and contrast two works of literature, in this case two poems. This essay can discuss how the poems handle the same topic, use the same literary form and conventions, create characters, represent the authors' point of view, represent the social customs of the time period, and so on. Read the following Emily Dickinson poem and see if you can find any points of comparison and contrast between it and Whitman's "A Noiseless Patient Spider."

> *This is my letter to the World*
> *That never wrote to Me—*
> *The simple News that Nature told—*
> *With tender Majesty*
>
> *Her message is committed*
> *To Hands I cannot see—*
> *For love of Her—Sweet—countrymen—*
> *Judge tenderly—of Me*

Start by asking some questions.

1. What is the subject of the poem?
2. Is there a metaphor in the poem?
3. What possible connection could there be between Whitman and Dickinson?

## Finding a Unifying Theme

When beginning a comparison/contrast essay you should begin by deciding what the focus of your response will be. What is the general topic? In the case of the two poems above, the general topic might be the importance of poetry as the way a man or woman finds his or her connection to the world. Like Whitman, Dickinson understands that feeling connected and understood by the world around her is very significant. When she writes, "This is my letter . . . " *this* refers to her poem and possibly her poetry in general. She calls her poem a *letter* and it is this metaphor—the comparison of her poetry to a communication with the world in general—which is at the center of the poem's meaning. By calling her poem a letter she implies that she is looking to communicate with someone (the world) through her poetry. She goes on to say that she is writing to someone (the world) who has never answered her before and so, like Whitman's patient spider, Dickinson is also patiently waiting to connect to the world. Like Whitman, she also sees poetry as the way to accomplish that connection. Unlike Whitman, she does not proclaim success. She simply suggests that "Her message is committed to hands she cannot see" (her audience, perhaps years in the future) and she asks that Nature's message, interpreted by Dickinson, be tenderly received. Whitman asks that we read his poetry and note his presence. He doesn't concern himself with our judgment of him or his work. Dickinson, on the other hand, asks that we read her and note her, but she recognizes that we will also judge her.

In short, both poets view poetry as a powerful and intense opportunity to express their connection to the world of the present and the future and while Whitman proclaims success and happiness, Dickinson seems only hopeful that her poetry will have a future audience.

## Apples and Apples

It is very important when developing a comparison/contrast essay that you compare apples with apples and oranges with oranges. For example, compare theme with theme, symbol with symbol, characters with characters, setting with setting, and so on. In the two poems above, the basis for the comparison was the common theme. The comparison of metaphors was an obvious second choice.

## Appropriate Textual Evidence

After you have found the common theme and the common elements for comparison/contrast, you must make sure that you choose appropriate textual evidence to support your claims. For example, in the discussion above, it was important to cite the specific words and phrases to support the statements that were made.

# THESIS STATEMENTS

When writing about poetry, whether a comparison/contrast of two or more poems or an analysis of just one, you start your essay with an introductory paragraph that asserts a thesis statement. Similar to the thesis statements we have discussed in the previous chapters, a thesis statement for poetry analysis, for any literary analysis, states exactly what you intend to develop in the body of your piece.

As you respond to the two poems above, a thesis statement might look something like this:

> Both Walt Whitman and Emily Dickinson view their poetry as their legacy to the world. They use metaphors to declare to the reader that they expect that their poetry, like all poetry, is a powerful expression of their unique personalities. Despite major thematic similarity, there are differences in the way the poems are written, the metaphors they use, and the conclusions they reach.

Now try looking at the following two poems. See if you can identify a common theme. What are the similes and metaphors? What is the tone and mood? What are the lines or words you appreciate the most? Can you write a thesis statement that summarizes your conclusions about the poems' similarities and differences?

WAR IS KIND
   By Stephen Crane

*Do not weep, maiden, for war is kind.*
*Because your lover threw wild hands toward the sky*
*And the affrighted steed ran on alone,*
*Do not weep.*
*War is kind.*

*Hoarse, booming drums of the regiment,*
*Little souls who thirst for fight,*
*These men were born to drill and die.*

*The unexplained glory flies above them,*
*Great is the battle-god, and his kingdom—*
*A field where a thousand corpses lie.*

*Do not weep, babe, for war is kind.*
*Because your father tumbled in the yellow trenches*
*Raged at his breast, gulped and died,*
*Do not weep.*
*War is kind.*

*Swift-blazing flag of the regiment,*
*Eagle with crest of red and gold,*
*These men were born to drill and die.*
*Point for them the virtue of slaughter,*
*Make plain to them the excellence of killing,*
*And a field where a thousand corpses lie.*

*Mother whose heart hung humble as a button*
*On the bright splendid shroud of your son,*
*Do not weep.*
*War is kind.*

**1.** To whom is the author speaking? List the three specific groups he addresses.
**2.** Does he really mean that war is good? Explain how he contradicts himself.
**3.** Would you say that Stephen Crane is pro-war or anti-war? Why?
**4.** What line or lines speak to you most clearly?
**5.** Who do you think says, "War is kind?"

Now compare Crane's poem to:

BEAT! BEAT! DRUMS!
    By Walt Whitman

*Beat! beat! drums!—blow! bugles! blow!*
*Through the windows—through doors—burst like a ruthless force,*
*Into the solemn church, and scatter the congregation,*
*Into the school where the scholar is studying;*
*Leave not the bridegroom quiet—no happiness must he have now with his bride,*
*Nor the peaceful farmer any peace, ploughing his field or gathering his grain,*
*So fierce you whirr and pound you drums—so shrill you bugles blow.*

*Beat! beat! drums!—blow! bugles! blow!*
*Over the traffic of cities—over the rumble of wheels in the streets;*

*Are beds prepared for sleepers at night in the houses? No sleepers must sleep in those beds,*

*No bargainers' bargains by day—no brokers or speculators—would they continue?*

*Would the talkers be talking? Would the singer attempt to sing?*

*Would the lawyer rise in the court to state his case before the judge?*

*Then rattle quicker, heavier drums—you bugles wilder blow.*

*Beat! beat! drums! —blow! bugles! blow!*

*Make no parley—stop for no expostulation,*

*Mind not the timid—mind not the weeper or prayer,*

*Mind not the old man beseeching the young man,*

*Let not the child's voice be heard, nor the mother's entreaties,*

*Make even the trestles to shake the dead where they lie awaiting the hearses,*

*So strong you thump O terrible drums—so loud you bugles blow.*

**1.** To whom is the author speaking? Unlike Stephen Crane, Walt Whitman is not speaking directly to any person or group of persons. His audience is the drums and bugles of war and in telling them what to do, he is telling us of their consequences. List three or four consequences of the drums and bugles of war.

**2.** Explain how Whitman's poem could be read as a positive call to arms.

**3.** Would you say that Whitman is pro-war or anti-war? Why?

**4.** What line or lines speak to you most clearly?

Having answered these questions, see if you can use your responses to answer the following essay question:

In an essay of approximately 750 words, compare and contrast Stephen Crane's poem "War is Kind" with Walt Whitman's poem "Beat! Beat! Drums!" Be sure to identify each poem's theme (what the author is saying about the topic of war) and then use specific evidence from the poem to prove your points. Include discussion of the way each author uses repetition of words and/or phrases to give emphasis to his views.

_____

_____

_____

_____

_____

_____

**EXPRESS YOURSELF** WRITING ABOUT POETRY

There are many levels on which you can be asked to write about poetry. In particular, you could be asked to explain a poem's use of specific literary devices or discuss its theme. But no matter how detailed or specific your assignment, you should not begin until you feel confident that you know what the poet is trying to say. You must first connect with the poem's message before you can comment on its methods or its successes. For example, if you had not known that Emily Dickinson was talking about using her poetry as her voice to reach out to the world, would you have appreciated the way she chose her metaphor or expressed her need for recognition? If you had not stopped to consider that Whitman's spider was just his way of helping us to understand his vision of poetry, would you have been able to see beyond a spider and his web? And if you do not appreciate the irony in Crane's claim that war is kind, you will not be able to compare and contrast his vision of war as the awful consequence of politicians sending young men to die for causes they know or care little about.

In short, writing in response to poetry should begin with your careful and thoughtful reading and re-reading of a poem. You should start by identifying what the poem is about and then try to identify the details that support your interpretation. Ultimately, you should be able to bring your own experiences and attitudes to your reading so that you can fully agree or disagree with the poet.

Writing in response to prose, specifically fiction such as short stories, novels, parables, myths, and fables, is not unlike responding to poetry. You must first understand the literal significance of a story and then you can begin to probe its deeper meanings. In the next chapter we will look at two short stories to see how to respond to them.

# ELEVEN

# WRITING ABOUT PROSE (FICTION)

**JUST AS** writing about poetry requires that you read carefully and thoughtfully, so does writing about fiction. You must concentrate and ask questions as you read. You may have to make a list of important vocabulary words as you go along, or you may have to underline or take notes in the text of words and phrases you think are important to the story's meaning. This chapter will show you some important reading strategies that will help you become a better writer when responding to fiction.

**B**efore we even begin to examine a short story or novel, it is important to remember the four key elements of all fiction:

→ plot
→ characterization
→ setting
→ theme

The *plot* is the sequence of events that delivers the story. *Characterization* is how the characters of the story are portrayed. The *setting* is the place in which the story occurs. The *theme* is what the author is saying about the subject of the story. All four of these elements contribute to the story, but it is the theme of the story which is its heart and soul. Read the following short story by Kate Chopin. It is a very short story but it contains all the elements of good fiction. As you read, identify where the story takes place; underline the word or phrases that identify it for you. Next, underline the major characters' names and the words that describe them. Finally, try to tell what the story seems to be about. What is it saying about marriage? About love? About loyalty?

## The Story of an Hour
### By Kate Chopin

Knowing that Mrs. Mallard was afflicted with a heart trouble, great care was taken to break to her as gently as possible the news of her husband's death.

It was her sister Josephine who told her, in broken sentences: veiled hints that revealed in half concealing. Her husband's friend Richards was there, too, near her. It was he who had been in the newspaper office when intelligence of the railroad disaster was received, with Brently Mallard's name leading the list of "killed." He had only taken the time to assure himself of its truth by a second telegram, and had hastened to forestall any less careful, less tender friend in bearing the sad message.

She did not hear the story as many women have heard the same, with a paralyzed inability to accept its significance. She wept at once, with sudden, wild abandonment, in her sister's arms. When the storm of grief had spent itself she went away to her room alone. She would have no one follow her.

There stood, facing the open window, a comfortable, roomy armchair. Into this she sank, pressed down by a physical exhaustion that haunted her body and seemed to reach into her soul.

She could see in the open square before her house the tops of trees that were all aquiver with the new spring life. The delicious breath of rain was in the air. In the street below a peddler was crying his wares. The notes of a distant song which some one was singing reached her faintly, and countless sparrows were twittering in the eaves.

There were patches of blue sky showing here and there through the clouds that had met and piled one above the other in the west facing her window.

She sat with her head thrown back upon the cushion of the chair, quite motionless, except when a sob came up into her throat and shook her, as a child who has cried itself to sleep continues to sob in its dreams.

She was young, with a fair, calm face, whose lines bespoke repression and even a certain strength. But now there was a dull stare in her eyes, whose gaze was fixed away off yonder on one of those patches of blue sky. It was not a glance of reflection, but rather indicated a suspension of intelligent thought.

There was something coming to her and she was waiting for it, fearfully. What was it? She did not know; it was too subtle and elusive to name. But she felt it, creeping out of the sky, reaching toward her through the sounds, the scents, the color that filled the air.

Now her bosom rose and fell tumultuously. She was beginning to recognize this thing that was approaching to possess her, and she was striving to beat it back with her will—as powerless as her two white slender hands would have been.

When she abandoned herself a little whispered word escaped her slightly parted lips. She said it over and over under her breath: "free, free, free!" The vacant stare and the look of terror that had followed it went from her eyes. They stayed keen and bright. Her pulses beat fast, and the coursing blood warmed and relaxed every inch of her body.

She did not stop to ask if it were or were not a monstrous joy that held her. A clear and exalted perception enabled her to dismiss the suggestion as trivial.

She knew that she would weep again when she saw the kind, tender hands folded in death; the face that had never looked save with love upon her, fixed and gray and dead. But she saw beyond that bitter moment a long procession of years to come that would belong to her absolutely. And she opened and spread her arms out to them in welcome.

There would be no one to live for during those coming years; she would live for herself. There would be no powerful will bending hers in that blind persistence with which men and women believe they have a right to impose a private will upon a fellow-creature. A kind intention or a cruel intention made the act seem no less a crime as she looked upon it in that brief moment of illumination.

And yet she had loved him—sometimes. Often she had not. What did it matter! What could love, the unsolved mystery, count for in face of this possession of self-assertion which she suddenly recognized as the strongest impulse of her being!

"Free! Body and soul free!" she kept whispering.

Josephine was kneeling before the closed door with her lips to the keyhole, imploring for admission. "Louise, open the door! I beg, open the door—you will make yourself ill. What are you doing Louise? For heaven's sake open the door."

"Go away. I am not making myself ill." No; she was drinking in a very elixir of life through that open window.

Her fancy was running riot along those days ahead of her. Spring days, and summer days, and all sorts of days that would be her own. She breathed a quick prayer that life might be long. It was only yesterday she had thought with a shudder that life might be long.

She arose at length and opened the door to her sister's importunities. There was a feverish triumph in her eyes, and she carried herself unwittingly like a goddess of Victory. She clasped her sister's waist, and together they descended the stairs. Richards stood waiting for them at the bottom.

Some one was opening the front door with a latchkey. It was Brently Mallard who entered, a little travel-stained, composedly carrying his grip-sack and umbrella. He had been far from the scene of the accident, and did not even know there had been one. He stood amazed at Josephine's piercing cry: at Richards' quick motion to screen him from the view of his wife.

But Richards was too late.

When the doctors came they said she had died of heart disease—of joy that kills.

On its surface, the story is about a woman with a heart condition who learns that her husband has been killed. She goes to her room and is very upset, crying and remembering her husband. Then she cries out, "free," and she feels both sad because her husband is dead but also joy that she is now free to be herself. Then her husband comes in the front door. He hasn't been killed, and he is just coming home from work as usual. The woman has a heart attack and dies of shock.

Sounds simple enough but there are some questions we need to ask.

**1.** What is Louise Mallard's opinion of marriage? Can you find the line or lines that suggest it?

_____

_____

_____

**2.** Why does Louise Mallard suddenly stop crying? Can you find the place in the text?

_____

_____

_____

**3.** How does she feel about her future as a widow? Can you underline the place?

_____

_____

_____

**4.** How do Louise's sister and his friend, Richards, feel about the Mallard's marriage?

_____

_____

_____

**5.** Why is there so much description of what is outside the window when Louise is alone in her room?

_____

_____

_____

**6.** Why did the author make the story so short?

_____

_____

_____

**7.** Explain how Louise can feel joy and sadness at the same time.

_____

_____

_____

**8.** Do you see any irony in this story? (Irony is the difference between the actual result of a sequence of events and the normal or expected result.) Can you write a brief summary of what you think the message of this story is and how the author uses irony to establish it? What is the author trying to tell us about marriage? About relationships? About the way we judge people and ourselves? Try writing a thesis statement and then developing two or three paragraphs with supporting details and textual evidence.

_____

_____

_____

_____

_____

_____

_____

_____

_____

_____

_____

_____

_____

_____

_____

_____

_____

_____

_____

_____

_____

_____

_____

_____

_____

_____

**9.** Are there any words which you need to look up—such as *importunities*?

_____

_____

_____

**EXPRESS YOURSELF**  WRITING ABOUT PROSE (FICTION)

See if your answers match these.

1. We learn from the story that Louise and Brently probably had a relatively good marriage—she "had loved him," at least "sometimes," and he had "never looked save with love upon her." But to Louise, no amount of love can erase the "crime" of marriage (paragraph 14). Louise realizes that self-assertion is "the strongest impulse of her being" (paragraph 15). In her marriage, however good it may have been, there was always Brently's "powerful will bending hers in that blind persistence with which men and women believe they have a right to impose a private will upon a fellow-creature" (paragraph 14). A marriage requires both partners to consider not just their own desires but also the desires of the other, and Louise believes that the most important thing is to be free to do as one pleases.

2. Though Louise often loved Brently, now that she is no longer a partner in a marriage, she is free to live her own life. When she stopped crying, the word that Louise whispers "over and over under her breath" in the room is "free" (paragraph 11). She says "[t]here would be no one to live for her during those coming years; she would live for herself" (paragraph 14).

3. Louise looks forward to her future. When she realizes that she will be free in the years ahead, she "opened and spread her arms out . . . in welcome" (paragraph 13). Her excitement is also demonstrated in paragraph 20. When Louise finally comes out of the room, she "carried herself unwittingly like a goddess of Victory." Though she will miss Brently (she "knew that she would weep again when she saw the kind, tender hands folded in death"), she prays that "life might be long" so that she can enjoy "all sorts of days that would be her own" (paragraph 19).

4. Louise's sister (Josephine), Richards, and the doctors all believe that Louise locks herself in the room out of grief and despair. Josephine worries that Louise "will make herself ill" (paragraph 17) and begs her to come out of the room. Josephine and Richards break the news of Brently's presumed death very gently (paragraph 1) so as not to upset her too much. They believe that because she loves him so much, this news will upset her greatly. In fact, the story suggests that Josephine and Richards think the Mallards have a good marriage and that Louise was a happy wife. Finally, Louise's happiness at the prospect of living for herself now that she is a widow is her secret; the others do not know how she really feels. If the others did know, they might think she was an ungrateful and selfish wife.

5. Outside her window, Louise sees an "open square" in which "the tops of trees . . . were all aquiver with the new spring of life" (paragraph 5). She smells the "delicious breath of rain" in the air and hears "countless sparrows . . . twittering in the eaves." The "new spring of life" in the trees represents the new life that Louise will have now that she can live for herself. The rain symbolizes the life-giving force of water, and birds, because of their ability to fly, are often a symbol of freedom. Further, their singing ("twittering") represents the happiness that Louise feels.

6. In the span of just two pages, Louise Mallard's life takes three dramatic—and, in the end, fatal—turns. First, she learns that her husband has been killed in a train accident. Instead of feeling grief, however, she learns that she is actually happy—happy to be able to live only for herself. Just as she begins to embrace her new life, however, she discovers that she will not be free after all. Having tasted freedom for a very brief moment, she realizes that she will continue to be a "prisoner" in her marriage. Chopin made the story so short to show how quickly and dramatically one's life can change.

7. We expect that a wife would be distraught when she finds out her husband has been killed in an accident. But we assume (like Josephine, Richards, and the doctors) that this wife was happily married.

That wasn't the case with Louise. That's not to say that she had a *bad* marriage. As far as we can tell, Brently never hurt her—he didn't beat her or cheat on her or put her down. She says that he "looked only with love upon her."

But the fact that they had a pretty good marriage makes it harder to understand how she could be so happy that he was dead. Is she a "monstrous," selfish person? Well, not really. The fact is that for Louise, the "strongest impulse of her being" was "self-assertion"—the ability to do what she wanted without having to bend her will to someone else's. In her mind, any marriage, no matter how good it is, is a "crime" because in a marriage, both partners "believe they have a right to impose a private will upon a fellow-creature."

Chopin probably would not write the same story today, since women have a lot more respect and have much more equality in our society than they did in her time. But then again, marriage is still marriage. Even if both partners are more equal today than they were in her time, there's still the problem that her story points out: a marriage forces two people to give up some of their freedoms in order to live together. Of course there are benefits to this. But if you really love someone, how can you ask them to give up their right to assert their true selves?

**8.** "The Story of an Hour" is filled with irony from start to finish. Chopin creates this ironic tone in two ways: through the plot and by letting readers see what's going on in Louise's head.

The plot of the story is simple but powerful. In the beginning, everyone thinks that Brently Mallard is dead. This news causes his wife Louise to come to a profound and disturbing realization. She's not really sad; as a matter of fact, she's glad. She's happy to be free. But here's the twist: Brently *isn't* really dead, and when he comes home, to everyone's surprise, his arrival kills Louise. Chopin adds to the irony by showing us that poor Louise had never felt more alive than when she realized she was free.

By letting us see what Louise is thinking, Chopin creates a tension that further increases the irony. "Free! Body and soul free!" Louise whispers. We can hear those whispers, but the other characters in the story—Josephine, Richards, and the doctors—cannot. We know that what really kills Louise is the fact that her husband is still alive. For a moment, she thought she was free to live her own life, but all too quickly her freedom is taken away from her. Because her freedom is so important to her (she recognized self-assertion as "the strongest impulse of her being"), this shock is enough to kill her. Thus, the final phrase in the story, "joy that kills," is particularly ironic. The joy that killed Louise was the joy she felt up in the room, not the joy that she felt when she saw Brently.

This tone reflects real life in many ways. Our lives can change so quickly, and very good and bad things can be set into motion because of an innocent mistake. More importantly, the irony in the story shows us that we often don't understand people or ourselves. We often have certain assumptions about how people feel or should feel in certain situations. But often those assumptions and expectations are wrong. And those assumptions can make people feel trapped and even hopeless. For example, Louise had "only yesterday . . . thought with a shudder that life might be long."

Maybe it's a little bit callous of Louise to feel such joy at the death of her husband. But maybe Chopin is suggesting that it's equally callous of us to judge her without knowing who she really is and why she feels this way. By using irony and letting us glimpse the real workings of Louise Mallard's mind and heart, "The Story of an Hour" tells us that things are not always what they seem and we should always look carefully before coming to conclusions about people and their relationships.

Following is a short story by Mark Twain, a noted American author. Read it carefully, and make notes in your notebook when you think you've discovered something significant about the characters or the plot. Remember, when you are finished reading you will be answering questions and writing about the story. See if you can't anticipate what you might need to include in your analysis at the end of your reading.

## LUCK

### By Mark Twain

It was at a banquet in London in honor of one of the two or three conspicuously illustrious English military names of this generation. For reasons which will presently appear, I will withhold his real name and titles and call him Lieutenant-General Lord Arthur Scoresby, Y. C., K. C. B., etc., etc.

What a fascination there is in a renowned name! There sat the man, in actual flesh, whom I had heard of so many thousands of times since that day, thirty years before when his name shot suddenly to the zenith from a Crimean battlefield, to remain forever celebrated. It was food and drink to me to look, and look, and look at the demi-god; scanning, searching, noting: the quietness, the reserve, the noble gravity of this countenance; the simple honesty that expressed itself all over him; the sweet unconsciousness of his greatness—unconsciousness of the hundreds of admiring eyes fastened upon him, unconsciousness of the deep, loving, sincere worship welling out of the breasts of those people and flowing toward him.

The clergyman at my left was an old acquaintance of mine—clergyman now, but had spent the first half of his life in the camp and field and as an instructor in the military school at Woolwich. Just at the moment I have been talking about a veiled and singular light glimmered in his eyes and he leaned down and muttered confidentially to me—indicating the hero of the banquet with a gesture:

"Privately—he's an absolute fool."

This verdict was a great surprise to me. If its subject had been Napoleon, or Socrates, or Solomon, my astonishment could not have been greater. Two things I was well aware of: that the Reverend was a man of strict veracity and that his judgment of men was good. Therefore I knew, beyond doubt or question, that the world was mistaken about this: he was a fool. So I meant to find out, at a convenient moment, how the Reverend, all solitary and alone, had discovered the secret.

Some days later the opportunity came, and this is what the Reverend told me:

About forty years ago I was an instructor in the military academy at Woolwich. I was present in one of the sections when young Scoresby underwent his preliminary examination. I was touched to the quick with pity, for the rest of the class answered up brightly and handsomely, while he—why dear me, he didn't know anything, so to speak. He was evidently good, and sweet, and lovable, and guileless; and so it was exceedingly painful to see him stand there, as serene as a graven image, and deliver himself of answers which were veritably miraculous for stupidity and ignorance. All the compassion in me was aroused in his behalf. I said to myself, when he comes to be examined again he will be flung over, of course; so it will be simply a harmless act of charity to ease his fall as much as I can. I took him aside and found that he knew a little of Caesar's history; and as he didn't know anything else, I went to work and drilled him like a galley-slave on a certain line of stock questions concerning Caesar which I knew would be used. If you'll believe me, he went through with flying colors on examination day! He went through on that purely superficial "cram," and got compliments too, while others, who knew a thousand times more than he, got plucked. By some strangely lucky accident—an accident not likely to happen twice in a century—he was asked no question outside of the narrow limits of his drill.

It was stupefying. Well, all through his course I stood by him, with something of the sentiment which a mother feels for a crippled child; and he always saved himself—not just by miracle, apparently.

Now, of course, the thing that would expose him and kill him at last was mathematics. I resolved to make his death as easy as I could; so I drilled him and crammed him, and crammed him and drilled him, just on the line of question which the examiners would be most likely to use, and then launched him on his fate. Well, sir, try to conceive of the result: to my consternation, he took the first prize! And with it he got a perfect ovation in the way of compliments.

Sleep? There was not more sleep for me for a week. My conscience tortured me day and night. What I had done I had done purely through charity, and only to ease the poor youth's fall. I never had dreamed of any such preposterous results as the thing that had happened. I felt as guilty and miserable as Frankenstein. Here was a wooden-head whom I had put in the way of glittering promotions and prodigious responsibilities, and but one thing could happen: he and his responsibilities would all go to ruin together at the first opportunity.

The Crimean War had just broken out. Of course there had to be a war, I said to myself. We couldn't have peace and give this donkey a chance to die before he is found out. I waited for the earthquake. It came. And it made me reel when it did come. He was actually gazetted to a captaincy in a marching regiment! Better men grow old and gray in the service before they climb to a sublimity like that. And who could ever have foreseen that they would go and put such a load of responsibility on such green and inadequate shoulders? I could just barely have stood it if they had made him a cornet, but a captain—think of it! I thought my hair would turn white.

Consider what I did—I who so loved repose and inaction. I said to myself, I am responsible to the country for this, and I must go along with him and protect the country against him as far as I can. So I took my poor little capital that I had saved up through years of work and grinding economy, and went with a sigh and bought a cornetcy in his regiment, and away we went to the field.

And there—oh dear, it was awful. Blunders?—why he never did anything but blunder. But, you see, nobody was in the fellow's secret. Everybody had him focused wrong and necessarily misinterpreted his performance every time. Consequently they took his idiotic blunders for inspirations of genius. They did, honestly! His mildest blunders were enough to make a man in his right mind cry; and they did make me cry—and rage, and rave, too, privately. And the thing that kept me always in a sweat of apprehension was the fact that every fresh blunder he made increased the luster of his reputation! I kept saying to myself, he'll get so high that when discovery does finally come it will be like the sun falling out of the sky.

He went right along, up from grade to grade, over the dead bodies of his superiors, until at last, in the hottest moment of the battle of —————— down went our colonel, and my heart jumped into my mouth, for Scoresby was next in rank! Now for it, said I; we'll all land in Sheol in ten minutes, sure.

The battle was awfully hot; the allies were steadily giving way all over the field. Our regiment occupied a position that was vital; a blunder now must be destruction. At this crucial moment, what does this immortal fool do but detach the regiment from its place and order a charge over a neighboring hill where there wasn't a suggestion of an enemy! "There you go!" I said to myself; "this is the end at last."

And away we did go, and were over the shoulder of the hill before the insane movement could be discovered and stopped. And what happened? We were eaten up? That is necessarily what would have happened in ninety-nine cases out of a hundred. But no; those Russians argued that no single regiment would come browsing around there at such a time. It must be the entire English army, and that the sly Russian game was detected and blocked; so they turned tail, and away they went, pell-mell, over the hill and down into the field, in wild confusion, and we after them; they themselves broke the solid Russian center in the field, and tore through, and in no time there was the most tremendous rout you ever saw, and the defeat looked on, dizzy with astonishment, admiration, and delight; and sent right off for Scoresby, and hugged him, and decorated him on the field in presence of all the armies!

And what was Scoresby's blunder that time? Merely the mistaking his right hand for his left—that was all. An order had come to him for fall back and support our right; and, instead, he fell forward and went over the hill to the left. But the name he won that day as a marvelous military genius filled the world with his glory, and that glory will never fade while history books last.

He is just as good and sweet and lovable and unpretending as a man can be, but he doesn't know enough to come in when it rains. Now that is absolutely true. He is the supremest ass in the universe; and until half an hour ago nobody knew it but himself and me. He has been pursued, day by day and year by year, by a most phenomenal astonishing luckiness. He has been a shining soldier in all our wars for a generation; he has littered his whole military life with blunders, and yet has never committed one that didn't make him a knight or a baronet or a lord or something. Look at his breast; why he is just clothed in domestic and foreign decorations. Well, sir, every one of them is the record of some shouting stupidity or other; and, taken together, they are proof that the very best thing in all this world that can befall a man is to be born lucky. I say again, as I said at the banquet, Scoresby's an absolute fool.

1. How does the narrator feel about Scoresby? Can you find the line(s) in the text which confirm your opinion?

_____

_____

_____

**2.** Why did the narrator's conscience bother him so much? Can you find the line(s) or words in the story which confirm your idea?

_____

_____

_____

**3.** Why did the narrator buy a *cornetcy* (a rank in the army) to go to war? Can you find the line(s) or words which tell you?

_____

_____

_____

**4.** How does the narrator feel about luck?

_____

_____

_____

**5.** How do you feel about Scoresby? Would you want to be in his regiment in the army? Would you want to be him?

_____

_____

_____

Now take your answers and see if they can help you to write a 750-word essay on the following topic:

In Mark Twain's story "Luck" we never meet the main character, Scoresby, yet we come to know him, and the narrator, very well. Describe both of these characters and tell how Twain uses them to establish his own attitude about military power and success in general.

_____

_____

_____

_____

_____

**EXPRESS YOURSELF** WRITING ABOUT PROSE (FICTION)

# QUESTIONS ABOUT LITERATURE

In general there are two types of questions that your teacher will pose about literature: short answer and essay. Short answer questions can take the form of true/false, multiple-choice, or any question type for which there is a definite right or wrong answer. These questions are almost always literal and they are almost always concerned with plot and setting. That is, they require you to have very specific, detailed information from the text. Another way to describe a literal question is that the answer can always be found in the text. For example, "What is the name of Louise Mallard's husband?" is a literal question. The answer is right in the story.

But all good tests will also require that you go beyond basic textual facts to interpretation. These questions are called figurative or interpretive questions and unlike literal questions, they are almost always concerned with characterization and theme. You must know the details from the text but these questions ask you to use those details to draw conclusions and opinions based on them. "Why did Louise die at the end?" This question has several possible answers. Literally, she had a bad heart, and the shock of seeing her dead husband killed her. But figuratively, or interpretively, she died because she was also shocked to realize that she really was glad he was dead and then disappointed that he was alive. This isn't stated in the text. It is *implied* and therefore, it is an interpreted response.

Good interpretive questions will lead you to use textual details in your responses, and you will always score more points if you quote words or lines from the text to support your opinions. For example, to say that the narrator in the story, "Luck," was genuinely alarmed that Scoresby would kill thousands of young men because of his stupidity would become much more powerful if you quoted the line from the story that said the narrator, "thought his hair would turn white" he was so alarmed.

On most high stakes tests for high school graduation you will be asked to read short fiction such as the short stories above and respond to short answer questions and then short essay questions. The short answer questions usually give you all the information you need to answer the essay part, and it is a good strategy to read the questions before you read the text so that you'll know what to look for as you read. Once you have answered the short answers, the essay part—often called open-ended or short response—should be clearly outlined for you.

# TWELVE

# WRITING ABOUT DRAMA

**WRITING ABOUT** plays is similar to writing about other forms of literature. You have to be alert to details of plot, setting, and characterization. But because plays rely solely on dialogue to convey their messages, reading drama and writing about it is unique. This chapter will show you how to interpret characterization and theme based on dialogue.

Plays are not written to be read. Plays are written to be performed. They are meant to be seen. Fortunately, with good video and DVD and some wonderful adaptations of performances for the screen, many of the plays that you are required to read in school are also available for you to see on your TV screen. There is, however, nothing like seeing a play performed live. In either case, video or stage, the opportunity to see and hear the play enhances the reading of it. There are two reasons for this.

First, plays rely on dialogue, the simple exchange of conversation between people, or in the case of certain plays, soliloquies. But as you well know, your mother can call you for dinner, and it is the tone of her voice, her pitch, and her body language that conveys her mood. The same words, minus the tone of her voice and her body posture, can have many different meanings. When you read dialogue you have to be able to read between the lines, so it is imperative that any play be read at least two, if not three times. "What?" you might say. "I have to read something twice when I hated it once?" Yes. And your teacher(s) have probably already set it up that way for you. You read it over at night for homework but then you read it again, carefully, with nuance, in class.

Consider the soliloquies in the play *Hamlet*, by William Shakespeare. As you well know, a soliloquy is a speech delivered by a character to reveal his innermost thoughts and feelings. It is not dialogue in the sense that it is an exchange between two or more characters, but it is the way the playwright discloses a character's thoughts without the benefit of an elaborate textual explanation such as is possible in a short story or novel. Consequently, the soliloquy is a very important window into the main character's heart and mind.

In *Hamlet* there are seven soliloquies, all focused on the major themes of the play and designed to reveal how Hamlet develops as a man confronting enormous moral, social, and political obligations. Read the following soliloquy, and see how much you can learn about Hamlet's character and mental state.

> To be, or not to be, that is the question:
> Whether 'tis nobler in the mind to suffer
> The slings and arrows of outrageous fortune
> Or to take arms against a sea of troubles
> And by opposing end them. To die, to sleep—
> No more; and by a sleep to say we end
> The heart-ache and the thousand natural shocks
> That flesh is heir to; 'tis a consummation
> Devoutly to be wish'd. To die, to sleep;
> To sleep, perchance to dream—ay, there's the rub;
> For in that sleep of death what dreams may come,
> When we have shuffled of this mortal coil,
> Must give us pause—there's the respect
> That makes calamity of so long life.
> For who would bear the whips and scorns of time,
> Th' oppressor's wrong, the proud man's contumely,
> The pangs of despis'd love, the law's delay,
> The insolence of office, and the spurns
> That patient merit of th' unworthy takes
> When he himself might his quietus make
> With a bare bodkin? Who would fardels bear,
> To grunt and sweat under a weary life,
> But that the dread of something after death,

*The undiscovere'd country, from whose bourn*
*No traveller returns, puzzles the will,*
*And makes us rather bear those ills we have*
*Than fly to others that we know not of?*
*Thus conscience does make cowards of us all,*
*And thus the native hue or resolution*
*Is sicklied o'er with the pale cast of thought,*
*And entrerprises of great pitch and moment*
*With this regard their currents turn awry*
*And lose the name of action.*

**1.** Find the line or lines which tell us that Hamlet is thinking about being dead.

_____

_____

**2.** Find the line or lines which suggest that he views dying as the easy way out of a problem.

_____

_____

**3.** Find the line which suggests that Hamlet is worried about what may come after death.

_____

_____

**4.** How does Hamlet characterize death?

_____

_____

**5.** How does Hamlet regard his conscience?

_____

_____

**6.** What do the lines, "And thus the native hue of resolution/Is sicklied o'er with the pale cast of thought" mean?

_____

_____

**7.** Explain the metaphor for death that Hamlet uses in the opening lines.

_____

_____

**8.** What is the resolution to the opening question?

_____

_____

How is reading this soliloquy different from reading it as if it were a poem? Without the benefit of the plot and setting it could be a poem. But it does have a setting, a plot sequence, and characterization to breathe life into it. Once you know that Hamlet is considering suicide because he is so upset about his situation, and that he is considering murdering his uncle to avenge his father's death, you read these lines about death and dying with much more power and intensity. Indeed, the playwright gives us a far more powerful presentation about the conflict between conscience and behavior because these lines are spoken by a man, not merely written.

Thus, when we listen to this man feeling the need to kill himself because life has been so brutal to him, we hear his pain. When he talks of "sleep" as a metaphor for death, and he considers "dreams" as a logical consequence of sleep therefore even in death there may be something beyond peace, we hear his fear. And when he tells us that "conscience" makes us all cowards, afraid to die because we know how guilty we have been in life and therefore uncertain of the "dreams" that will follow us to eternity, we become partners with him.

We come to understand that "the native hue of resolution," or the resolve to kill oneself or even kill another, is "sicklied o'er" with "thought" and after considering it seriously, Hamlet has lost "the name of action."

Notice that in answering the questions presented above, an analysis of the soliloquy has started. Notice, too, that in answering the questions direct quotes from the lines have been given. In responding to drama, using the words of the characters is extremely important. They are the keys to supporting our interpretations.

The second important difference between plays and other forms of literature is the compressed nature of the action. Often, plays take place in a matter of days in the lives of its characters. Rarely do they take place over the course of years. They frequently open in the middle of things, giving us background as we go along, and then take us with them to the end of whatever crisis is occurring.

We are invited in to witness action in the daily lives of these people, often just like ourselves. We listen to their conversations and soliloquies, and observe the consequences of their words and actions. Ultimately, it is our reaction to their words and the reactions of the characters on stage, which will guide our interpretation of the play. In the case of Hamlet, the young prince who has returned home from school to find a murdered father and a remarried mother (to his father's brother no less) we read much between the lines. We read the soliloquy above and understand why he would even consider suicide; his pain is almost unbearable.

Now consider this essay question based on the soliloquy above:

In his "To be, or not to be" speech, the young Prince Hamlet carefully considers the boundaries between life and death. Using specific lines from the speech, show how Hamlet's thinking evolves from the opening question to its concluding answer.

Thus, when responding to any piece of literature, it is careful reading, and attention to textual detail, that will make you a better writer about literature. Stories, poems, and plays are not inkblots, subject to random interpretation. They are carefully crafted works of art, which provide all the necessary details to support valid opinion. On the next two pages is a rubric that might be used to evaluate a literary essay.

\* \* \*

If you look carefully at the rubric that was adapted from a New York State Comprehensive English Regents Examination Rubric used to score a literary essay, you will notice that the most important qualities of an essay are meaning, development, and organization. Language use and following the conventions of standard written English are important but they are at the bottom of the rubric.

The reference to *meaning* in the rubric is whether or not you have grasped the implied or inferential complexities of the story and its characters. Did you understand the subtleties of characterization? Did you notice how the author created tone and mood? For instance, with the Hamlet soliloquy, were you able to see that his despair is heightened for us because he seems obsessed with death and dying? He is not just sad. He is despondent and morose.

The reference to *development* in the rubric concerns whether or not you have developed your interpretation(s) with specific details from the text to prove that your interpretation is accurate and not just an inkblot reaction. Did you use specific quotes? Were you able to identify literary devices such as irony or satire and show how they contributed to your interpretation? Did you recognize figurative language such as similes and metaphors, and could you use them to reinforce your opinion? Can you connect Hamlet's reference to dreaming and conscience?

The reference to *organization* in the rubric is specific to the organization of your essay. Does it have a good introduction with a clear thesis statement (focus)? Do you have body paragraphs that are logically presented with good transitions? Does your conclusion restate your thesis and secure your interpretation as valid?

The reference to *language use* in the rubric means your language not the author's. Is your vocabulary varied? Sad is not the only word for Hamlet. Are you repetitious? Are your sentences varied or are they all simple sentences? Notice that there isn't much difference between the 5 and 4 paper in this category. But look at 3 and 2. The reference to *ordinary*, *imprecise*, *vague*, and even *inappropriate* language are traps that are easy to fall into. Even when you are confident that you understand a short story or poem to its very core, you can falter when trying to express yourself. Start trying to build your vocabulary so that you are have a repertoire of words from which to choose.

Finally, the reference to *conventions* in the rubric means exactly what it says: spelling, punctuation, paragraphing, grammar, and usage. A thoughtful, insightful interpretation of a literary piece can be doomed to a low grade if it is filled with mechanical or homonym (your/you're) errors. Paragraphs must be as organized as entire papers are organized, with topic sentences and supporting details. Be sure to carefully proofread and edit your final copy.

A last word about proofreading and editing. By the time you reach your junior and senior year in high school you will be writing in timed test situations, many of which will have enormous consequences—high school graduation being just one. During those tests you will not have the benefit of peer or teacher review

RUBRIC FOR LITERATURE ESSAYS

| Quality | 5 | 4 | 3 | 2 | 1 |
|---|---|---|---|---|---|
| | The response: | The response: | The response: | The response: | The response: |
| **Meaning:** The extent to which the response identifies the author's theme and purpose for writing and responds to the tone and mood of the piece. | • Accurately identifies literary devices and details which convey the author's meaning and purpose. • Interprets the complexity of thought in the literature. | • Accurately identifies some of the details that contribute to the meaning and purpose of the piece. • Limited interpretation. | • Limited understanding of the meaning and purpose of the piece. • Relies on literal information. • Provides little insight to the implied meaning. | • Brief, sketchy discussion of the meaning. • Poor understanding of the inferential meaning. | • Demonstrates poor to no understanding of the message and purpose. |
| **Development:** The extent to which the discussion is elaborated through specific references to the author's choice of genre, detail, figurative language, and other literary devices. | • Makes effective use of generalization, specific references and relevant quotations from the piece to support discussion. • Develops ideas fully, using a wide range of relevant textual support. | • Supports discussion with appropriate generalizations, specific references, and relevant quotations from the text. • Develops ideas fully, using a wide range of relevant textual support. | • Supports discussion with specific references to the piece, with main ideas usually distinguished from supporting details. • Develops ideas simply, using a limited range of textual support. | • Mentions some ideas and information from the piece, with some attempt to distinguish main topics from details. • Includes limited range of details that may be irrelevant or inaccurate. | • Conveys vague or unsupported ideas, or presents random list of details. • Includes inaccurate and/or irrelevant use of references from the piece. |
| **Organization:** The extent to which the response exhibits | • Establishes a clear, original, relevant focus for the response. • Exhibits a logical and | • Establishes a clear and relevant focus for the response. • Exhibits a logical and | • Establishes an appropriate focus for the essay. • Exhibits a discernible | • Establishes some direction for the response, but organization is tentative. | • Lacks a focus for the response and shows little or no evidence of organization. |

**EXPRESS YOURSELF** WRITING ABOUT DRAMA

RUBRIC FOR LITERATURE ESSAYS (continued)

| Quality | 5 | 4 | 3 | 2 | 1 |
|---|---|---|---|---|---|
| | The response: | The response: | The response: | The response: | The response: |
| paragraph development, transitions, and logical progression of ideas. | coherent organizational structure through effective use of such devices as introduction, conclusion, and transitions that contribute to the cohesion of the whole. | coherent organizational structure through the use of such devices as an introduction, conclusion, and transitions. | coherent organizational structure. | | |
| **Language Use:** The extent to which the response exhibits effective use of words, sentence structure, and sentence variety to convey ideas. | • Conveys ideas and information in original and precise language with a noticeable sense of voice. • Makes effective use of sentence structure and length to convey ideas. | • Conveys ideas and information in original and precise language. • Shows consistent use of sentences that are varied in length and structure. | • Uses ordinary language or language from the piece to convey ideas and information. • Relies on sentences that are unvaried in length and structure. | • Relies on ordinary, often imprecise language to convey ideas and information. • Relies on sentences that lack variety in structure and length and may be constructed incorrectly. | • Includes some vague, inappropriate, and/or incorrect language. • Relies on run-ons or sentence fragments. |
| **Conventions:** The extent to which the response exhibits conventional spelling, punctuation, paragraphing, grammar, and usage. | • Exhibits correct spelling, punctuation, paragraphing, grammar, and usage. • Error-free. | • Exhibits generally correct spelling, punctuation, paragraphing, grammar, and usage. | • Exhibits minor errors in spelling, punctuation, paragraphing, grammar, or usage that do not interfere with communication. | • Exhibits errors in spelling, punctuation, paragraphing, grammar, or usage that may interfere with communication. | • Exhibits error in spelling, punctuation, paragraphing, grammar, or usage that often interfere with communication. |

to help you proofread or edit before you submit a final copy. But if you take advantage of the opportunity to peer review the work you do every day, to become alert about how you write and the mistakes you commonly make, as well as the suggestions of others about how to improve your work, you will become more astute at proofing your own test work.

There are several peer review sheets at the end of this book which you should try to use routinely before you hand in a written assignment. You will notice that they all refer to things like "thesis statement," "paragraph development," "word choice," and even "conventions." You can modify them to match the requirements of a particular assignment. For example, if the assignment requires that you write about Hamlet's soliloquy and select at least three references to death and dying, then you can add that criteria to the peer review sheet to make sure your reader picks up whether or not you have addressed this in your finished piece.

Finally, there is no magic bullet to help you express yourself. Reading insightfully, acquiring good vocabulary, recognizing logic, and preparing well-organized papers are all skills that have to be worked at.

# TIPS FOR PEER REVIEW

Real writing takes shape during revision. You'll want to use the peer review forms found here to check and revise your work to make it the best it can be.

## Peer Review 1

**1.** Does the first paragraph get your interest? What details, information, quotation accomplishes this? What, if anything, is still needed?

_____

_____

**2.** At the end of the first paragraph, do you know what the thesis is? Express the thesis in the author's words or your own.

_____

_____

**3.** As the author tells the story, are the details vivid and interesting? Point out several good ones.

_____

_____

**4.** Is there a logical time sequence? What transition words or phrases capture the sense of time?

_____

_____

**5.** Are more details needed anywhere? If so, explain.

_____

_____

**6.** Are there any good comparisons (similes and metaphors)? List them below.

_____

_____

**7.** Are you satisfied with the conclusion? Does it restate the opening? If you think it could be better, please write it out.

_____

_____

**8.** Do you see any serious grammatical errors? Circle the places where you think there is an error. Give suggestions for better wording.

_____

_____

## Peer Review 2

**1.** Does the introduction effectively identify the issue, engage the reader's interest, provide needed background, and provide the writer's thesis? How might the writer improve the introduction? Suggest a quotation, statistic, or anecdote.

_____

_____

**2.** If the introduction predicts the organization of the paper, do the body paragraphs follow the thesis statement? Do you ever have trouble seeing the purpose or function of the paragraphs? Can you circle the transition words or phrases?

_____

_____

**3.** Identify places where the prose is confusing or unclear. In particular, look at abrupt transitions, gaps in arguments, tangled sentences, or other places where you get lost.

_____

_____

**4.** Is each paragraph well-developed? Is there a good topic sentence with at least three supporting sentences? Is there a clear transition from paragraph to paragraph?

_____

_____

**5.** Does the conclusion restate the introduction?

_____

_____

**6.** What are the main strengths of the paper? Underline one or more important phrases.

_____

_____

**7.** What are at least two changes the writer should consider making?

_____

_____

## Peer Review 3

**1.** What is the *thesis statement*? Copy it below.

_____

_____

**2.** How many paragraphs make up this essay?

_____

_____

**3.** Is the first paragraph an effective introduction? What introduction strategy does the writer use— that is, quotation, statistic, or anecdote?

_____

_____

**4.** Is each body paragraph adequately developed? What evidence is used to support the thesis? Is the evidence compelling? Select one or two pieces of supporting information that you think are very good.

_____

_____

5. Which parts of the essay do you find most effective? Cite a specific sentence, paragraph, or example to support your opinion.

_____

_____

6. What did you learn from this essay?

_____

_____

7. Make one suggestion for improvement.

_____

_____

8. Read over for the conventions of standard written English; circle errors, but do not make corrections. That is the writer's job.

_____

_____

## Revision Guidelines for Self Evaluation

Before submitting your work, check the following:

1. Can you underline your thesis statement?

_____

_____

2. Does each paragraph begin with a recognizable topic sentence that introduces a major point to be developed in the paragraph?

_____

_____

3. Can you identify transitional words or phrases in each paragraph?

_____

_____

**4.** Are your pronoun references clear?

_____

_____

**5.** Is your writing concise and exact? Do you use active voice where possible? Can any sentences be combined? Are you repetitious?

_____

_____

**6.** Can you substitute stronger vocabulary words anywhere?

_____

_____

**7.** Does your conclusion restate your thesis?

_____

_____

**8.** Have you checked the conventions of standard written English? Are there any comma splices? Run-on sentences? Sentence fragments? Homonym errors?

_____

_____

# B

# ANSWERS AND EXPLANATIONS

Following is a sample essay for the Supreme Court case essay on page vii.

## Answer

Throughout U.S. history, the United States Supreme Court has dealt with many major issues. Three major cases that have had profound impact on society and law enforcement are *Brown v. Board of Education* (1954), *Miranda v. Arizona* (1966), and *Roe v. Wade* (1973). In each case, the decision, the circumstances, and the significance changed the way we think and act.

In *Brown v. Board of Education*, decided by the Supreme Court in 1954, segregation in American education became illegal. Prior to 1954 the law stated that "separate but equal" facilities were acceptable for separating blacks and whites. In another Supreme Court case called *Plessy v. Ferguson*, decided by the Supreme Court in 1896, the court said that as long as railroad cars were the same, blacks could be forced into separate cars from whites. From 1896 to 1954 this "separate but equal" rule was applied by those states wishing to maintain other segregated facilities and the rule was applied to school systems.

However, in 1954, the family of a black student named Brown sued the city of Topeka, Kansas, claiming that separate educational facilities provided for blacks were inherently inferior to those provided for whites and therefore they were merely "separate" and not "equal." The attorneys for Brown argued that the Fourteenth Amendment to the Constitution of the United States, which includes the "equal protection clause," was being violated because the rights of black students to a quality education were not being protected in the same way that white students' rights were being protected. The doctrine of separate but equal was therefore unconstitutional. The Supreme Court unanimously agreed. As a result of this decision no state could enforce segregation in its schools and public education in the United States changed forever. This was a major legal decision that had profound effects on American society.

In the case of *Miranda v. Arizona*, law enforcement was changed. In 1963 a man named Miranda was arrested for a serious crime, and he confessed after the police questioned him. When his lawyers appealed his conviction they argued that because he was not told his rights, anything he said couldn't be used against him at his trial. In other words, because he wasn't told that he had the right to an attorney, the right to remain silent, or the right to have an attorney provided for him, he had been denied the rights given to him by the Fifth Amendment to the Constitution. This amendment outlines that everyone has the right to "due process" of law and specifically that a person's rights, liberty, and property cannot be violated without a proper trial.

The Supreme Court was not unanimous in its decision. But the majority said that defendants couldn't be convicted in federal or state courts if they are denied the due process of law from the moment they are taken into custody. Part of that due process is being reminded of their rights under the Fifth Amendment to the Constitution. These rights are now called *Miranda Rights,* and since the court decision in 1966 anyone arrested in the United States, even foreigners, must be read their five basic rights. Law enforcement changed forever with this decision.

In the case of *Roe v. Wade,* a woman's right to terminate an unwanted pregnancy was upheld. In 1973 the Supreme Court found that Texas laws that made abortion a crime were unconstitutional because they violated a woman's right to privacy and her right to "equal protection under the law" as found in the Fourteenth Amendment.

In 1963 a young, single, unwed mother wanted to end her pregnancy. She couldn't find a doctor to help her because in Texas it was a crime to perform abortions. The woman sued, and her case went all the way to the Supreme Court. Many people think that *Roe v. Wade* gives women an open option for abortion anytime in their pregnancies. But the court decision said that states could have laws about when an abortion could be performed; however, they just couldn't say it was a crime in any and every case. In the *Roe v. Wade* case all they said was that in the first trimester a woman should be able to decide for herself; it was a privacy issue. *Roe v. Wade* changed society because we are still arguing about abortion; in fact it is one of the most controversial issues we face today.

In conclusion, three Supreme Court case decisions have had major impact on society and law enforcement.

## A Task-Specific Rubric

Following is a rubric which is used to measure an essay like the Supreme Court case essay.

| Category | 6 | 5 | 4 | 3 | 2 | 1 |
|---|---|---|---|---|---|---|
| **Use of data** | • Always uses accurate and relevant data. | • Consistently uses accurate and relevant data. | • Uses mostly accurate and relevant data. | • Mixes accurate and inaccurate, relevant and irrelevant data. | • Uses mostly inaccurate and irrelevant data. | • Uses almost no accurate or relevant data. |
| **Plan of Organization** | • Always demonstrates a logical and coherent plan of organization. | • Consistently demonstrates a logical and coherent plan of organization. | • Develops the assigned topic using a general plan of organization. | • Addresses the assigned topic, but demonstrates weakness in organization and may include digression. | • Attempts to develop the assigned topic, but demonstrates a profound weakness in organization and may include several digressions. | • Minimally addresses the assigned topic and lacks a plan of organization. |
| **Development of ideas** | • Always develops ideas fully and clearly, using appropriate examples, reasons, details, explanations, and/or generalizations. | • Consistently develops ideas fully, using appropriate examples, reasons, details, explanations, and/or generalizations. | • Demonstrates satisfactory development and expression of ideas through the adequate use of support materials. | • Demonstrates weakness in the development and expression of ideas with little use of support materials. | • Demonstrates profound weakness in the development and expression of ideas, with little use of support materials. | • Does not use support materials in the development or expression of ideas. |

(Taken from New York State Regents Examination for grading student essays)

## Explanation

Try your hand at rating the Supreme Court Case Essay.

**1.** Notice that what is most important, in a content-based essay such as the Supreme Court Case essay, is the accuracy and relevancy of the data that is used. This makes sense because it is measuring your retention and understanding of information.

_____

_____

_____

**2.** The second most important quality of the essay is its organization. Does it have a beginning, middle, and an end? Is it unified? Do the paragraphs make sense?

_____

_____

_____

**3.** The third, most important category is the development of the ideas. Do you just cite data or do you explain it?

_____

_____

_____

**4.** How would you rate the sample essay?

_____

_____

_____

## Answers

**1.** This is a well-developed essay that has a clear introduction that restates the question and uses it to create a thesis statement.

**2.** The body paragraphs follow the organization declared in the first paragraph and each case is explained for its decision, circumstances, and historical significance.

**3.** Accurate and relevant details are used to support the claims made in each of the paragraphs, and the writer never loses sight of what the assigned topic is.

**4.** The essay is well-organized and fully develops the ideas using appropriate reasons and explanations.

Answers to the questions on pages 13-14, "The Food Pyramid"

## Short Answers

1. **c.** This would be the best title because the article is concerned with eating healthy food. Shopping for it is emphasized in the second paragraph.
2. **b.** Stay in the outer aisles because that is where the healthier foods are located.
3. **a.** This is the correct choice because the food pyramid doesn't tell you what to eat or what not to eat. It just suggests quantities.
4. **d.** This is the correct choice because the passage talks about the junk food being located in the inner aisles.
5. **c.** This is the correct choice. None of the other choices are stated in the passage.
6. **a.** This is the best choice because "The Food Pyramid" is the basis of the entire passage.
7. **a.** This is the best choice because the entire passage reminds you what you *should* eat and how you *should* shop, and it provides lots of information to convince you.
8. **b.** This is the correct choice. It cites "The Food Pyramid" which is a recognized as current scientific evidence.

## Open-ended Questions on page 14

1. The author uses "The Food Pyramid" to prove that it is healthier to shop the outer aisles of the grocery store. She shows that the foods on the bottom of the pyramid, are healthier foods than the ones found in the outer aisles.
2. The author would want everyone to have a copy of "The Food Pyramid" because he or she feels strongly that eating healthy foods is important. The author also demonstrates the "The Food Pyramid" is a very helpful, easy to read diagram.

## Answer to Essay on page 17, "Industrialization"

Industrialization has caused many problems for the nations of the world. Most nations are responding to the problems by trying to find solutions. Many are working together to be sure that our world remains a healthy and productive place to live.

For example, in 1992 the United States and 34 other industrial countries met in Rio de Janeiro to discuss world environmental concerns brought about by industrialization. They created a prioritized list to help identify and then direct efforts to addressing them. Two of the most important concerns were encouraging efficient resource use, and protecting global and regional resources, including the atmosphere, oceans and seas, and living marine resources.

Two nations that are ahead of their neighbors in responding to the call for energy efficiency are Britain and Denmark. British Petroleum President John Browne announced that BP would be stepping up investments in solar energy, and Denmark has been working for the past ten years to generate electricity from wind power and the combustion of agricultural wastes. These are very important efforts to help conserve resources and protect the environment.

Another concern of the world's nations is that developing countries are working against the trend to conserve resources. As emerging nations struggle to move from simple farming to manufacturing, they need the attention and help of the rest of the world. The United States Department of Energy projects that carbon emissions from the expansion of developing nations will eclipse efforts to reduce emissions unless policies are put into place to stop it. One example of this is the projection that by the year 2015 China will surpass the United States as the world's leading emitter.

Furthermore, unless attention is directed to countries such as Japan, which consumes ten times as much of the world's resources as the average Bangladeshi, human consumption and waste will have devastating effects on available resources. Japan and Bangladesh have the same population numbers but Japan consumes excessively. Clearly one of the goals of the Rio pact is to establish guidelines and policies to bring awareness to countries like Japan.

The future of the environment is clearly in danger and the nations of the world are only beginning to take notice. Industrialization brings wealth and comfort but it also brings carbon emissions and disregard for finite resources. We can predict the future, but can we prevent disaster?

Use the rubric on page 143 to rate this essay. Did it answer the question? Does it use evidence from at least four of the documents? Is it organized? Are the facts and details relevant to the arguments? How does your essay compare?

## Answer to "Smoking" on page 26

For many years, physicians and tobacco companies have known that smoking is linked to serious long-term health problems. Yet the tobacco companies keep marketing cigarettes to young people, hoping to develop future consumers. The money incentive far outweighs the quality of life issues. But it is time for big tobacco to recognize its role in contributing to the health of the future. Teenage smoking has long-term consequences, which will cause irreparable harm because tobacco is an addictive substance, causes major organ damage—such as heart disease—and causes oral cancers.

First, the concept of addiction must be considered. For years the tobacco companies have denied that nicotine is an addictive substance. They don't want their product compared to alcohol or heroin. But just like illegal drugs, nicotine is addictive. Ask anyone who has tried quitting. In fact, according to the American Cancer Society, nine out of ten people who start smoking will become addicted, and only three of ten who try to quit are successful. Compare that ratio with the following data, also provided by the American Cancer Society: one out of every ten people who starts drinking will become alcohol dependent and six out of ten who use cocaine will become addicted. Indeed, quitting heroin is easier than quitting tobacco. Yet big tobacco's big lie doesn't stop them from producing cigarettes and marketing them to young consumers all the while denying that their product is harmful.

Big tobacco also knows the serious health issues related to their product. Tobacco use causes an immediate physical response—sweating, rapid pulse, increased hand tremor, insomnia, nausea or vomiting, physical agitation, anxiety, to name a few. But it is the long-term effects that are deadly. The number one risk factor for coronary artery disease, better known as heart attack, is cigarette smoking. Nicotine causes the linings of the arteries to become sticky so that plaque, and cholesterol, adheres to the walls of the arteries and blockages develop. But heart attack is only one deadly consequence.

Serious lung disease is directly linked to tobacco use. Lung cancer and emphysema are the result of tobacco consumption, and both are painful, deadly diseases. The cost to families in emotional stress and dollars is almost incalculable. Watching someone suffer from lung disease and knowing that it was preventable if cigarettes had not been marketed causes anger and regret. It also makes parents try to impress the no smoking message on their children. But the cigarette manufacturers are way ahead of us. Statistics tell us that despite efforts to curtail teenage tobacco use, it is on the rise. In 1998 the Center for Disease Control and Prevention noted that 24.1% of adults were smokers, and the highest incidence of smoking was among 18–44-year-olds. Asked when they began smoking, 87% said when they were 15 or younger!

If that were not bad enough, young people are also experimenting with smokeless tobacco, commonly called "chew." They seem to think it is less harmful than smoking. But it isn't. Oral cancers of the tongue, lip, and jaw are the direct result of chewing tobacco. Yet ballplayers do it and young men imitate them and, like cigarettes, the warnings are just perfunctory. If people took them seriously, there would be a decline in tobacco sales, and we all know that isn't true.

The American Academy of Family Physicians says that decreasing the rate of cigarette smoking in our young people should be the number one health objective of this country. If that is true, and we know that all the empirical data proves smoking to be so deadly, why are tobacco companies still in business? Why can we buy their product in any convenience store on any street corner?

The answer is simple. Money. We cannot count on the tobacco companies to advise its customers of the deadly effects of their product but we can put a dent in the number of teens who smoke by passing on the important information that smoking is an addictive, disease-causing habit.

Now compare this essay against the rubric on page 143. Does it satisfy the requirements for accurate, reliable, and relevant data? Are the ideas developed with examples? Is the essay organized with clear paragraphs? See if you can use one of the peer review sheets in Appendix A to evaluate the piece closely.

## Answers for pages 31-32

1. Please send a catalog at your earliest convenience.
2. The catalog I requested has not yet arrived.
3. My transcript has an error that needs correction.
4. Being on time and prepared to work are requirements for success in class.
5. Clean clothes and a neat appearance are a must for all employees.

## Sample Persuasive Topics

School-related:

1. censorship of your school newspaper
2. school dress codes
3. zero tolerance
4. attendance policies
5. exit exams for a diploma
6. more money for sports, music, field trips
7. more money for textbooks, computers, other supplies
8. support for trips abroad
9. McDonald's in the cafeteria
10. open or closed campus

General Interest:

1. increased funding for prescription drugs
2. raising the driver's license age
3. mandatory road testing for senior citizens
4. abortion laws
5. school prayer
6. gun control
7. death penalty
8. state lotteries
9. cell phone restrictions
10. cigarette legislation